SHE WANTED MORE

POORNA BELL
SHE WANTED MORE

REIMAGINE YOUR FUTURE AND LIVE BY YOUR RULES

First published in the UK in 2026 by LEAP
An imprint of Bonnier Books UK
5th Floor, HYLO, 105 Bunhill Row,
London, EC1Y 8LZ

Copyright © Poorna Bell, 2026

All rights reserved.

No part of this publication may be reproduced, stored or transmitted in any form or by any means, electronic, mechanical, photocopying or otherwise, without the prior written permission of the publisher.

The right of Poorna Bell to be identified as Author of this work has been asserted by her in accordance with the Copyright, Designs and Patents Act, 1988.

This book is a work of Non-Fiction. Some names have been changed to respect the privacy of those mentioned.

A CIP catalogue record for this book is available from the British Library.

Hardback ISBN: 9781785122835
Trade Paperback ISBN: 9781785122842

Also available as an ebook and an audiobook

3 5 7 9 10 8 6 4 2

Design and Typeset by Envy Design Ltd
Printed and bound by CPI (UK) Ltd, Croydon CR0 4YY

Every reasonable effort has been made to trace copyright holders of material reproduced in this book, but if any have been inadvertently overlooked the publishers would be glad to hear from them.

The authorised representative in the EEA is
Bonnier Books UK (Ireland) Limited.
Registered office address:
Block B, The Crescent Building
Northwood, Santry
Dublin 9, D09 C6X8, Ireland
compliance@bonnierbooks.ie

www.bonnierbooks.co.uk

Mama,
You used your bones to grow mine, a heart for a heart, your breath as the billows.

It has taken time to realise the scale of your love, almost half a century to understand the sacrifices.

But now we are here, and should you wish for the moon, should you wish for anything more, and should it ever be in my power to give, it is yours.

DISCLAIMER

All women in the survey and who messaged in online have been given pseudonyms to protect their anonymity.

Joy shakes me like the wind that lifts a sail,
Like the roistering wind
That laughs through stalwart pines.
It floods me like the sun
On rain-drenched trees
That flash with silver and green.

I abandon myself to joy—
I laugh—I sing.
Too long have I walked a desolate way,
Too long stumbled down a maze
Bewildered.

Clarissa Scott Delany, poet, essayist and social worker associated with the Harlem Renaissance movement

god forbid a girl doesn't lower her standards and dies alone in a little cottage, filled with fresh flowers and home-baked goods, best friends and indoor plants, too many books, pretty art, clean bathrooms, low lights, great support and no one to take from her the love that was never meant for anyone else but herself.

Emma Beames, writer

CONTENTS

PROLOGUE — 1

CHAPTER ONE
We Climb with Courage — 5

CHAPTER TWO
Let's Do Some Weeding — 23

CHAPTER THREE
Harnessing Power, Anger and Change — 41

CHAPTER FOUR
Marriage and Long-term Relationships: the Good, the Bad and the Truthful — 59

CHAPTER FIVE
Breakups, Shakeups and WTFs — 87

CHAPTER SIX
The Renegotiation of Mother and Motherhood — 111

CHAPTER SEVEN
Otherhood: the Shift in Identity Around Not Being a Parent   133

CHAPTER EIGHT
Dating, Expectations and the Joop-scented Reality   153

CHAPTER NINE
Sex and Sexuality   173

CHAPTER TEN
Introducing the Climacteric! (AKA All Things Menopausal)   203

CHAPTER ELEVEN
Reimagining the Conversation Around Ageing   221

CHAPTER TWELVE
Role Models and Conversations with Our Mothers   243

CHAPTER THIRTEEN
Freedom, Healing and Joy   259

ACKNOWLEDGEMENTS   287

REFERENCES   291

PROLOGUE

Summer had always been my favourite season, but there was one year in which it was gobbled whole and not even the bones remained. That was ten years ago, when my husband Rob died. My memories of that time are a nebulous skein of eating, sleeping, going to work, seeing my loved ones, and the in-between, when I didn't need to be anything to anyone. I would lie on my bed and look out at the sliver of blue sky held in the corner of the window.

I spent a long time in this liminal state. Time moved differently there. It would contract like a concertina so that the day of Rob's death felt like yesterday, and then quickly expand so that the grief seemed infinite. Even though there was evidence the world around me was growing, the vines of jasmine curling under my window, pots of ferns holding green lace in their tightly bunched fists, I felt as if my life was over.

I was thirty-four. I lost the ability to think about the future and so I never imagined I would have a middle age. Worrying about turning forty feels pointless when you don't expect to get there.

No living thing can remain awake and in stasis for ever, and when I emerged back into the world, I knew immediately that I was a different person. My past self was buried on a New Zealand winter's day alongside my husband, and my future self was yet to be decided.

The world knew what had happened to me, and so it left me alone for a bit. I didn't feel the pressure to be anything other than a creature trying to survive from one day to the next, but eventually that changed. When I started to show signs of recovery, flecks of happiness that began sealing the cracks in my life, I was considered match-fit to be entered back into the game a couple of years later.

This was the game of everything that tells a woman what she is, and how to be. If you follow the rules, you will be safe and happy and adored. Be thin, eat less, find a man, have kids, don't complain, don't age, be grateful, don't ask for too much money, stay small, be scared, don't brag, be quiet. If you do all the things we're telling you to do, your life will have purpose!

Except, I *did* do most of those things. It didn't unlock the doors of acceptance, or untold riches, and I almost lost myself trying to make it all work. So I remained sceptical, until middle age approached in the form of my fortieth birthday, a blank page in a book I thought would have ended several chapters earlier.

And then I became angry. Instead of being encouraged to feel gratitude and liberation for overcoming grief and

SHE WANTED MORE

embracing life, I was told there was a new problem in addition to all the old problems: I needed to overcome ageing. From here on out apparently, things would only get worse – my body, my mind, my life. It was the beginning of the end.

Except, I'd already been through an end. And this wasn't it. I was being told my best days were behind me, when in fact they had been some of my worst days. Nearly a decade of my thirties veiled in a mist of pain and longing. And now I was being told that what I had to look forward to was decay, and whatever scraps of youth I could hold on to?

No thanks. I'm no longer playing a game by someone else's rules.

I don't accept that I am powerless to change things, or that I should wait for the right time to be brave. I don't accept that getting older is something to vanquish, defeat, conquer. I don't accept that the default of womanhood is sacrifice, and that your purpose is to burn yourself up like a candle so that everyone but you can benefit from the light and warmth. I don't accept that I have lived this long to be told my best years are now behind me. I don't accept being defined by anyone else's hands when I hold both pen and script.

I have seen death, and I have seen life. And upon choosing the latter, there is no force on earth, no will – not even my own, refracted through societal expectations – that will keep me from living it to its fullest. There is more to life than what we've been told. And I want more, I want more, I want more.

CHAPTER ONE

WE CLIMB WITH COURAGE

This is a story you may have heard before. A woman meets a man, and she is excited, so excited, because he seems different to the rest, because he messages her back *on the same day*. They discuss travel bucket lists and on a wet Tuesday evening, he slips in 'we' and, although she really tries not to, she imagines them together, building a life that is holidays and pastries and lazy Sunday mornings. He says he loves her ambition, but frowns when she tells him about a win she had at work. He talks endlessly about the things they'll do together but when she tries to pin him down as to *when,* he's always going through a busy period. He makes a comment about what she wears when she tries something new but then says *it's just a joke!* when her face falls. She tries not to notice the deadness behind her friends' eyes when she talks about him. Red is a colour she cannot see when the beginning is painted in sunshine and yellows, turning all of it green.

This is a story you may have heard before. A woman has been told that she needs to get to a certain level before she can be promoted, but no one seems to know what this level is. *We don't have the budget,* her boss says, *but when I leave, I'll make sure your name is in the running as my successor. If you take on this extra role for no extra money, I'm sure you'll be a shoo-in.* She waits, and waits, patiently waiting for someone to notice, to do the right thing, because she's grateful, so grateful to be considered, and then one day her colleague says, *hey, have you met our new boss yet?*

This is a story you may have heard before. A woman loves her children, she really does, and during the holidays, she cancels her hair appointment because she doesn't have time to do that *and* drive all the way to the farm shop to buy her children a special chicken so that she can make a roast. She picks up all the treats they like so that they can have a film day, limbs splayed in a heap like they once did back when they were cubs. They pile into her kitchen and fling open the fridge door. The accusations fly. *Why didn't you buy this? WHY did you get that?* Her split ends look at her as if to say, *what did you expect?* The chicken says nothing because it is a chicken.

This is a story you may have heard before. A woman has a screensaver of a place she has always wanted to visit, a rocky canyon where the colours of the rainbow are pressed into stone, rippling like a cart of ice cream tipped on its side. She has dreams of this place, from scaling the ridges to pouring sand out of her shoes. But she can't possibly go alone because it's embarrassing. Eventually this desire fossilises into regret and longing and she wishes she hadn't cared so much about what other people might think.

This is a story you **have** heard before. It's about a woman who shrinks her desires and dreams to the smallest possible measurement so that she isn't inconveniencing other people with her needs and wants. A woman who doesn't want to ask for too much because she doesn't want to seem greedy. A woman who spends so long hoping for a full plate, that she doesn't notice that others have feasted on her joy, her grace, her glow, while she waited for scraps.

This is a story **you will be hearing now**. The story of many women, including myself, who will tell you about the moment we refused to accept less, and demanded more from ourselves and from others. More honesty, more love, more compassion, more bravery, more time, more peace, more sanity.

This is the story of women who have evolved their marriages, and the women who have left them. Women who are living alone and have no wish to live with someone ever again. Women who are changing the parameters of how they co-habit with their partners. Women who are building communities to grow old in together. Women who are choosing to parent differently, who are making powerful choices for themselves as mothers. Women who are not just accepting that they have to do things a certain way because that's how they have always been done. Women who aren't necessarily making radical changes, but whose lives are evolving. They are not a minority or fringe radicals, but part of a growing movement of women – especially in their forties, fifties, sixties and beyond – who are reimagining what life can be like when you learn to think for yourself, and to think differently. Moreover, these are not isolated stories; they gain power from being told collectively.

They will tell you that it is never too late to try something new, to start again, to write yourself something different, to pull as much joy into your life as you can. I feel the force of these women and their stories rippling underneath tectonic plates, a wave of joy and fury, changing their world and, in doing so, the world around them. It feels vital, and necessary, to gather these stories, because the star maps of what life is supposed to look like after a certain age are blank. Too many of us are looking back to the past, instead of looking up to the sky to imagine what the future could look like.

* * *

This book has been in the making for nearly six years, kindling gathered into a heap ready for the bonfire.

While it is for anyone of any age, I wanted to focus on women in their forties, fifties, sixties and seventies, because these were the women who'd had to change the most in their lives, given the societal pressures and expectations they had been raised with. It also felt important to change the narrative we have around ageing and empowerment – particularly for girls and younger women.

The first match was struck just before my fortieth birthday, when I could no longer bear the doom spiral of my peers who were also turning forty. It was constant – how it was the end, how much our backs hurt, how tired we were all the time, how we could no longer access fun and silliness in the same way we did when we were younger. (Now at forty-five, I yearn to go back in time and slap myself with a slipper. And not even a nice little ballet pump – platform Crocs, perhaps.) Alongside this was a sense that the year of being thirty-nine was running out fast, sand whistling through an egg timer. All of us were normally rational people, and no one could quite identify why there was such a specific fear around turning forty; for some reason it just lurked in the shadows like a bogeyman.

We started 2020 thinking this was our biggest problem, and then we had a whole damn pandemic, which razed claws through our sense of safety and security so that we saw it for what it was: an illusion. I had a slightly different year, in that I got the Big Bad Covid in March 2020, and that turned into ten months of post-viral fatigue, also known as Long Covid. I spent my fortieth birthday in December with much bigger problems than the spectre of wrinkles and back pain: would I ever recover? Would I ever get my energy back? This was something I spent hours thinking about alone on the sofa, spread-eagled like a human smear, while everyone else did jumping jacks in their living rooms and talked about homemade cocktails.

Two months after my birthday, I made a full recovery, and my first thought – while surrounded by all these notions of what a forty-something person does or looks like – was: *FUCK THIS.* I had lost too much time to navel-gazing and wasn't going to be dragged back into the murk of feeling unsure about who I was. I might not know everything, but I knew almost immediately upon turning forty that I felt more confident and certain about my career than I had ever done, that how I looked counted for fuck-all if my body wasn't well, and that there was power to be had in the clarity around time and value.

I started to get a sense of the emerging power of older women in 2020, when I was researching my book *Stronger,* and came across a number of mature amateur athletes who were doing things like pole vaulting and heptathlon well into their seventies and eighties. A couple of years later, I started to see an increase in women visibly subverting expectations around fitness. These were not blonde twenty-somethings in Gymshark clothing, nor were they pro athletes. One woman, Roshni Devi Sangwan, also known as Weightlifting Mummy on Instagram, shared her journey of lifting at the age of sixty-eight in her salwar kameez. Another woman named Betty Broadhurst talked about starting to learn Brazilian jiu-jitsu in her fifties and became a black belt in her sixties. Alongside this came the rise of the sixty-something fashion influencers, and then the sex influencers.

While their stories were inspirational, the second match was struck when I noticed a pattern emerging when talking with friends and hearing the same things come up again and again over dinner. The details of the story changed, depending on who was telling it, but it was the recurring tale of feeling stuck in their own lives, as well as struggling to advocate for themselves, whether it was around their relationships, friendships, appearance or careers. Aside from the antagonism they faced – which often centred around men – they would sometimes reveal things they dreamed of doing, only to talk themselves out of it.

SHE WANTED MORE

Circumstances and finance were sometimes to blame, but I didn't get the sense that those were the main blocks. The real problem was almost a form of self-sabotage. And interestingly, this lack of confidence and sense of *smallness* was something they would never accept for their female friends, or even a stranger. Consider how many drunk women in nightclub bathrooms have gone into battle for each other having only just met, united by nothing but shared toilet tissue passed under the door. They have reminded me of my worth when a man has crushed the magnificence in me.

When I ran a survey of over 1,000 women for this book to glean more insight into how they were feeling about their lives, I asked the question – *what is the one thing you want to change or add to your life?* As many as 74% of my respondents were over the age of forty.

Many women said: travel, moving abroad, changing or quitting jobs. One of the most popular responses was *move somewhere to be beside the sea*, and while I don't doubt the healing and restorative nature of the ocean, I also feel this is a metaphor for freedom. Others said they wanted more time, better sex, more sex, more money, financial independence, better friendships, fulfilling romantic relationships, to be seen and valued. The responses were varied, complex, wonderful. I felt I was being entrusted with the deepest part of their wishing.

Some of them were:

- I would buy a hobby farm and breed alpacas and make beautiful jumpers and blankets.

- Leave my husband and be with my lover. But this won't happen as we are both married and family is everything to us.
- Remove my children's father from our lives. Emotional abuse, in the eyes of the law, is hard to prove but the damage has been done. The three of us are strong.
- Build a multi-generational co-living community (not a commune) in London.
- Give my partner an ultimatum.
- Escape domestic abuse earlier. But I have made it!
- Take a lover. I miss sex. My husband has a low sex drive – he's extremely loving but I do miss sex.
- Stop my hoarding behaviour. I'm scared to let go.

When I asked what they wished for other women, one of the most powerful comments was: *Your dreams, desires and power are valid. You decide what enough is and where you belong.* I felt it all, these dreams and wishes that sit beneath the surface of our lives, these women who are out there, thinking they are alone, but connected like a constellation by the desire for more.

Women are not perfect creatures filled with love and light, but when we come together to help each other, we are unstoppable. I have seen it over and over again in my lifetime, from how we stand up for each other on public transport, to how we help each other move home in safety, how we show up with food, how we create initiatives so that other women can build their own lives, how we cheer each other on.

Any woman, no matter where she is from, wants to be

allowed to exist as she is, to do the things she loves and to be free. The fact that women persist in this goal, despite the horrors they face, is testament to a will and force that is formidable.

An enduring image is the Climbing Cholitas, or the *Cholitas Escaladoras*, a group of indigenous Aymara women in Bolivia, who have summited the highest peaks in the country, overcoming sexism by becoming climbers rather than settling for their assigned role as service staff. They also experience discrimination and scorn over their traditional dress, the *pollera*, and this is what they wear while climbing literal mountains, their colourful skirts, in pinks, yellows and greens, fluttering in the wind, softness against the unrelenting rockface.

Speaking at a UNESCO event, Lita González, a Bolivian mountain guide and founder of the Cholitas Escaladoras collective, said: 'We came together in fear, but climbed with courage. Wearing our traditional clothing, not knowing if we could. That's when I realized the strength was already there – it was in our blood.'[1] The capacity that women have for collective action, for friendship, for saying to each other, *I know you are scared but hold my hand and we can do it together*, is greater than anything this world tries to do to us.

There have been many times when a friend has been telling me about a problem in her life, and I've thought: 'I wish you could see what an incredible person you are. I wish you could see that there are a hundred different ways to be happy, and that you are deserving of joy. I wish I could tell you to stop accepting so little when you don't just deserve the moon, but the solar system that surrounds it.'

That's what this book is. I don't want to tell you how to live your life, but I want to help you figure out how to have a stronger voice within it. I want to ease any guilt you may feel around changes you might have to make, especially where they might involve your partner and/or children. I want you to see everything that is draining the battery in the background, that you hadn't even realised, so you have more freedom, time and energy. I want you, for once, not to have to justify how you're going to spend that extra time, or make it productive. In fact, I would *love* you to do some weird, silly shit with it.

Part of this is also personal. While I realise my circumstances are unusual – I'm a widow and I don't have children, which makes me a minority squared in my own age group – it's not about the specifics; rather it's about how I, like so many others, am questioning my life, and desires and dreams. As I navigate my forties, I am struck with a sense of power, but also freefall. Like many women doing the same in their fifties and sixties, there is no sense of what life 'should be like' at these ages because it already is so radically different to our mothers' generation.

Women aren't a monolith, and so another part of this reimagining of a different future will involve speaking to a number of experts, while others will speak to their own lived-in experience.

Sari Botton, who runs one of the most popular newsletters, *Oldster Magazine,* which has 68,000 subscribers and is a life-affirming read for people of all ages, told me: 'I've been learning that as they get older, women are less concerned with people's opinions of them, and, with that in mind, more eager to make choices that feel authentic to them, harsh societal judges be damned.

'They want to let go of the things they once chose under the influence of a patriarchal culture, and replace them with things that feel aligned with who they truly are. This can mean pursuing different kinds of work, different friendships and romantic relationships, new places to live, new creative pursuits.'

We are currently in an unprecedented time where women are creating art, writing about their experiences, sharing their lives on social media, and debunking the myths around being a woman, what gives us purpose, and getting older.

We are also in the midst of a global roar by younger women who are voicing how fed up they are with dating men, and how they are choosing to prioritise peace over constantly having their hopes dashed and being treated poorly. There have been endless conversations prompted by Lily Allen's album *West End Girl*, a raw capture of her marriage to the actor David Harbour. All you need to know about this album is that a man changed the rules of his marriage, then broke the rules regardless, and gave the woman just enough hope and crumbs of love that she wouldn't leave, while driving her almost to the point of relapse.

I wrote a piece on why it resonates with women, and the number of messages I received were staggering in their scope. These are not women breathy with youth, in the thrall of fandom. These are not women who are in non-monogamous marriages, nor are they famous, nor have they had their homes featured in *Architectural Digest*. This isn't really about the album, but the discourse and truth-telling it is sparking, and the beast slowly waking within us.

These are everyday women like you and me, who have reached the limits of what they will put up with. Who are awakening to what is stealing their power, and who want to reclaim their joy. They are fed up of having to squeeze their pain into smaller and smaller boxes, to constantly sanitise their feelings, and to cry a little quieter because it's ruining the mood.

Alongside this is the journalist Chanté Joseph's article entitled: 'Is Having a Boyfriend Embarrassing Now?' It went viral globally, sparking untold videos and think-pieces; marking an enormous shift in the consciousness of women, which is that having a man is no longer the ultimate life goal. We'll get into it later, but it doesn't mean removing men from your life, rather it means re-centring yourself; and that can range from your appearance to how you structure your relationship.

Interestingly, in the survey, when answering the question, 'What is most important in a life well-lived?', 93% of women in the survey said good friends, closely followed by good health. Family was 77%, while romantic relationships came in lower at 58%.

It also speaks to a new type of power being handed to single women, which is that they can feel empowered by their status rather than being written off as bitter and unloved. It speaks to a larger trend: tired of waiting for men to evolve, or for structural systems to change, women are exiting situations that don't serve them because their social status no longer hangs on having a man.

I've worked as a journalist in the UK for over 23 years, and during that time most of my work has focused on women's equality and women's issues. I pay close attention not just to the news, but also to the chatter that surfaces on social media. I don't just read the captions, I read the comments. I see what resonates with people, what moves them, what gets them angry. I add all these little pieces together and try to see the picture as a whole.

A journalist senses a zeitgeist shift like a dog smelling sausages, and I feel it in the air.

When I interviewed behavioural and data scientist Dr Pragya Agarwal, the author of *Sway: Unravelling Unconscious Bias*, she said that, while this type of change is happening in a relatively narrow spectrum of privilege, we are indeed making strides. 'In every generation, women have been trying or hoping to achieve more autonomy and there is a slight shift in how women are seeking to be more empowered. Women's mobilities are changing. Women's economic power is perhaps changing.'

In 2022, Morgan Stanley produced a report that focused on women's impact on the economy and said that by 2030, 45% of women aged between 25 and 44 will be single. They believe this is because women are delaying marriage, choosing to stay single, or divorcing in their fifties and sixties. They are also delaying childbirth (or refusing to rush into it until they find the right partner), and they are having fewer children. It's not that women are roundly rejecting marriage or the idea of having children, but evidence shows they are being more considered about it and are raising their expectations around what they want from a life partner.

I believe we are in the middle of a significant behavioural shift for women across many different areas, from relationships to careers, to how we take care of our bodies, how engaged we are in our own health, and, in terms of advocacy for ourselves, ownership of our anger, and generating change within our own lives. Women are starting to embody a much more truthful approximation of what we want from our lives, and there are women who need to know that this is possible, and to not settle for less or make fear-based decisions.

'As you look at your own mortality,' Dr Agarwal said, 'you might ask yourself: is this how I want to spend the rest of the years that I have? Women can maybe feel more able to say, this is what I need and this is what I desire, which they might not have done earlier in their lives, when they were trying to conform more to social and cultural norms and the expectations that were imposed on them. As we grow older, yes, there may be hormonal reasons [as to why this is], but I think it's more about socio-cultural reasons as to why we are less likely to conform to some of these expectations as we grow older.'

However, this change is far from accessible to all, and we still live at a time when women all over the world face many inequities. 'There is still no gender parity in terms of who has more power to make decisions, whether in a political domain, public domain, or domestic domain,' Dr Agarwal added.

SHE WANTED MORE

It is hard to write a book about the positives when a woman's voice cannot be heard in public in Afghanistan. When abortion rights have been decimated in the United States, and when insisting on the definition of a woman in the UK to exclude 0.01% of the population is apparently more important than tackling the sexual assault and domestic violence that women experience daily from cisgender men who make up 49% of the population.

The true scale of incel culture has also been unveiled thanks to the TV show *Adolescence*, which revealed that it affects boys much younger than previously thought. It pulled something ugly and necessary into the light – Gen Alpha and Gen Z might be more aware of mental health, and have a better grasp of sexual fluidity and racism, but they have a problem with misogynist radicalisation.

In a 2024 UK poll of 3,600 males between sixteen and twenty-nine, a majority thought feminism had done more harm than good, and that it was harder to be a man than a woman. And, in 2025, research conducted by Male Allies UK, questioning 1,000 boys across thirty-seven schools, revealed that 54% of boys think they have it harder than girls.[2][3] This is despite the fact that violence against women and girls is increasing, and has been declared a public health crisis in the UK – with girls more likely to experience sexual violence than boys, especially online.[4]

In 2025, we are about twenty years off achieving equal pay.[5] In the UK, 5% of women hold leadership positions in the tech industry – an industry that literally shapes how we think and live, now using AI, one of the most important technological advancements in centuries. There is a gender data gap especially around health, as highlighted by Caroline Criado Perez in *Invisible Women: Exposing Data Bias in a World Designed for Men* – women are more likely to be misdiagnosed for cardiovascular diseases because our symptoms differ from men's,[6] and there are numerous reports of women being rebuffed or dismissed after going to their doctors for help around peri-menopause and menopause.

Having read all this, it may seem as if the only solution is to commandeer a rocket and start life on a different planet. But there is one beacon of light shining through it all, which is that women are not putting up with it, and – where possible – they are creating their own systems to thrive in. They are protesting and campaigning, and they are digging deep into the idea of community. Many women jest about setting up a commune so they can spend the rest of their days eating cheese and sunbathing in peace, but some of us are serious about it. Women are engineering change at an individual level that feels unprecedented, and not all these changes are being made by wealthy women who have the means to do whatever they want. In the midst of all this darkness, I take comfort in that.

One of the most powerful demographics to embody this are women in their forties and fifties. It's undeniable that peri-menopause and menopause play a big part in stripping away the layers that may previously have made us more compliant, but, like Dr Agarwal says, I think that is only a part of it. We have tried being the 'having it all' generation, and have realised it's yet another bind and are rejecting it. And all those things combined mean we are arranging our lives a little differently from what came before.

Consider the powerful words of psychotherapist and author Jody Day, who does a lot of advocacy work for sixty-plus women. 'The fragmentation of female identity at menopause is a powerful initiation into a level of female maturity that our patriarchal society is not built for and does not tolerate,' she said.

'As we move away from being "fuckable" (that is, potentially fertile), we lose what power we may have been granted by the male gaze, and without the socially sanctioned identities of heterosexual partnerhood, motherhood and/or potential grandmotherhood, this lays bare how flimsy the structures are that we may have built our sense of self-worth and identity on. The awakening can be brutal and has the potential to be utterly transformative. I know that the life I'm living is beyond the wildest dreams of my female ancestors. It would seem that among those women who have the opportunity to reject the norms of patriarchy, many of them are.'

For anyone feeling overwhelmed by it all, this book isn't about encouraging women to leave their male partners, to undertake needless, dramatic change, or to push any agenda that creates silos. As someone who lives within society, I feel that empathy, education and compassion are critical foundation stones and, without them, we risk moving further apart from each other.

The intention is to get women thinking about a number of things, from how to pull deep joy into our lives, to how to spring-clean what isn't working, how to dream, how to create change, how to stop feeling stuck, how to want more and not feel guilty about it.

* * *

Before we go on this journey together, allow your sails to fill with the wise words of the brilliant bestselling author Marian Keyes, who is in her sixties. I love Marian for many reasons, but one of them is her admission that she shouts at men in the gym for grunting too loudly.

'Women are always told that their needs and their wants come last,' she told me. 'If you have children, they will always take priority, and that is very hard to argue your way out of. But it comes back to that thing of: we only have one life. We really do. I think most of us don't realise it. And we are allowed to be happier. We're allowed to explore. We're allowed to do things that we feel passionate and excited about. And we always wait for the right time, but the right time is never, ever going to magically appear. It simply won't.

'There will always be somebody else asking us to do something, and because of the way we're conditioned, we will think we have to do it. You're allowed to be selfish, because at the end of the day, when you deny yourself the things that you're passionate about, or the knowledge that you're curious for, the only person you're hurting is you. Why would you hurt you, when you are so generous to everyone else, and the world won't end? People might be surprised and people might be annoyed, but fuck them and their anger or disappointment or shock – it's not going to kill you. You have to back yourself, and you have to be your own best advocate.'

CHAPTER TWO

LET'S DO SOME WEEDING

In order to make space for something new to grow and to plant the seeds of courage required to push change through, we need to do some weeding. A weed isn't inherently bad, but – by definition – it is something growing where you don't want it to. It might be damaging its environment, or it might be strangling other plants as it aggressively snatches up water and nutrients. In some cases it may be obvious what needs to be uprooted, and in others a weed may put forth beautiful flowers to fool you into thinking it serves a function. But it doesn't. It needs to come out and be examined in the sunlight. To be asked the question: 'What, if anything, have you done for me?'

What are the weeds in our lives that strangle and shrink, that masquerade as useful plants? What is a lie – that has been packaged as the truth? We must take steps to replace it with something that will actually nourish and allow us to grow.

As women, this is vital work if we want a future where we are physically and mentally able to do the things we want, as well as lead lives that are fulfilling and peaceful.

I mention this for two reasons. The first is because I want younger women to question what they've been told, and to start asking themselves whether the things they have been led to believe they should want, around marriage, kids and careers, are what they truly want. The second is because we are experiencing a time when women are feeling stuck and angry because of the conflict between the ideologies we've inherited from past generations, and greater knowledge around our hormones, and the desire for something better.

I spoke to Betty Reid Soskin, a truly remarkable woman who is 103 years old and a civil rights activist in the United States. She became a US Park Ranger at 85, before retiring at 100, and advised me to 'always seek that wanting'. That we should always pursue the knowledge we need to evolve, because even when we think we've arrived at the answer, that answer will stagnate after a time.

I'd been drawn to Betty's story after watching a video of her talking about becoming a park ranger. I was taken aback, not just because of her age, but because she spoke about having lived so many different lives. I'd been feeling very sorry for myself and wondering if being in my forties would negatively impact the kind of work I did, and whether I had missed a window of opportunity around success. She elaborated on how many different versions of her had existed, from being an activist to being a singer-songwriter, being a wife and a mother, dealing with depression, and then her work in the parks. It made me feel as if I could change my life at *any* age – and have agency over it. There wasn't an invisible line drawn between who I was and who I wanted to be.

'People are scared of variety,' she said in a soft voice, talking to me on a videocall from her home, 'because they're scared of taking risks. I think that very often people want to keep their lives really safe and the same, as much as they possibly can. What ends up happening is they remove all the variety from it, and for me, the variety is what keeps me going.'

While tracing the root of your life, and the decisions you've made, back to their source, will need to be a process that is unique and specific to you, I am going to share a bit about my own life, and the weeding I needed to do.

* * *

It wasn't until I went to university that I understood that my family was unusual, especially my mother. Many of us have strong women in our families, women who have overcome great odds and experienced privations to give us the lives we have now, but my mother was my blueprint for not just accepting things as they were. This was important within the cultural context of being South Asian, specifically South Indian.

Apart from spending five years of my childhood in India (between the ages of seven and twelve), the rest of it was in the predominantly white suburbs of Kent. At university, I came into contact, for the first time, with other South Asians from different parts of the subcontinent. I quickly realised that in comparison to some of them, who came from strict, deeply patriarchal households, I had a father who never made me feel like there was one rule for girls, another for boys. Where he was still and calm, my mother was fiery and outspoken, and her brand of feminism was – in some regards – more important to navigating life than my actual degree.

One of my most significant memories of her was when I was around ten years old, attending an Indian wedding, bored out of my tiny mind. There was an open bar serving alcohol, except it wasn't considered seemly for women to drink in public, let alone go and get a drink. When my mother realised that only men were going to the bar, and that it would be frowned upon if she went on her own, she was outraged. She roundly rejected any difference in the treatment of men and women, and marched up to order a whisky and soda.

Although my mother had raised us 'not to take shit from anyone' (her words, not mine), and despite my specific South Indian community being matriarchal in its power structure, we all exist within a globally patriarchal system. The power of such a system is in its ability to limit, block and shrink you in ways that may not seem obvious. And it is built into everything.

While the goals of getting married and having children ostensibly came from my family and cultural upbringing, they were underpinned and reinforced by almost everything I watched on mainstream western TV. Growing up in the English countryside in a time before social media, when the most exciting thing to happen was a local festival where teenagers drank too much stolen booze and passed out under a tree, television was a portal into a much wider, more exciting world.

SHE WANTED MORE

It taught me a lot, and not all of it was good. For instance, the idea that all little girls dream of their wedding is revisionist history. When I asked other women what they dreamed about as girls, most of them said they dreamed of owning a stable of horses, being a superhero, being a doctor, taking part in the Olympics. In a lot of the TV shows I watched, having a boyfriend was considered the pinnacle of achievement, and this was reflected in films – except now it was about women 'convincing' men to put a ring on it, or women always trying to get in the way of their male partner having fun. This idea, that women were joyless and obsessed with marriage and kids, was fixed in our heads – we believed it, and men believed it too.

The award-winning poet Hollie McNish, whose subject matter spans womanhood, masculinity, politics and identity, perfectly encapsulates *why* we believed this narrative. 'I was looking back on the films and TV shows, songs and books that I got such a lot of lessons and inspiration from as a teenage girl and into my twenties,' she told me, 'and over 95% of the scripts and lyrics were written by men. Older men's words in the mouths of teenage girls and young women. Almost every single female character I looked to for inspiration, all the words she spoke, were scripted not only by an older guy, but often by guys who are now in prison for assault, abuse, and so on.'

Consider the hyperbolic extremes that women were written into: we were either fixated on 'trapping' a man, or if we were above the age of forty, we might as well be dead.

'I genuinely used to think that at forty, the world of sex and lust and love and adventure and respect would just stop,'

Hollie said. 'Like, you were a bit pointless. And then in my twenties I worked with a lot of women in their forties in a clothes shop, and they were having a time of it and I realised I'd basically been learning about women through old-man-scripted cheerleader films!'

When you consider the 2014 OkCupid study that showed men of every age are consistently attracted to women in their mid-twenties (it's okay – you can take a pause to swallow the yarf rising in your throat), while women tend to be attracted to men of a similar age to them, it is hardly surprising that forty-something women aren't the object of desire when they are written by men.[7] And there were other negative influences. Listening to how our grown-up neighbours and teachers talked disparagingly about women. Reading women's magazine features writing about the best ways to please your man. Going to weddings and community celebrations and having people say weird things like 'he's going to be your future husband' when you're only eleven and there happens to be a boy of a similar age in the vicinity. Seeing how a woman's value seemed to be measured in her proximity to a man, while a man's value was measured in how much he has. Fertilising all the thirsty little weeds in our garden with this grade-A shit.

When I thought about my teenage years, I remembered how we as girls would imagine ourselves getting married to whichever singer or actor we were obsessed with. I'm not sure straight boys were imagining themselves getting married to Pamela Anderson or Cindy Crawford – their fantasies seemed to mostly extend to sex. While I'm sure there were boys who felt constrained by the need to show sexual bravado, they seemed to have access to the full gamut of desire in a way that we did not.

Kate Bolick addresses this in her book, *Spinster: Making a Life of One's Own*. 'You are born, you grow up, you become a wife,' she wrote. 'But what if it wasn't this way? What if a girl grew up like a boy, with marriage an abstract, someday thought, a thing to think about when she became an adult, a thing she could do, or not do, depending? What would that look and feel like?'

When I entered my twenties I was hyper-focused on meeting the man of my dreams. Although I worried about whether my career as a fledgling journalist would ever take off, romance was front and centre. I had crushes and flings. A couple of good relationships. A bad relationship with a man who left his girlfriend to be with me, and as I basked in the exceptionalism of it all, he cheated on me with her. (I can't fault karma on that one.) I poured a lot of love and effort into men who lost interest once they had claimed me, and I behaved badly myself – careless with the hearts of people I knew were mine.

My parents were not the type of people to insist that I marry a South Asian man, although they would have liked it for the simple practicality of our cultures being similar. They needn't have worried – I had the same idea. However, the men I was dating in my twenties had been raised in households where they were encouraged to behave like entitled princes, while I had been raised in a household of queens. They expected me to shelve my needs or default to them just because they were men, and I couldn't.

Although I have since reconnected with South Asian men romantically in my forties and found them to be complex, funny, wonderful and accomplished (especially the ones who have worked on their emotional intelligence), my last proper relationship with a South Asian man finished on my twenty-fourth birthday, when we were arguing in Leicester Square at 1am. I'd lost him in a nightclub, only to find him on a different floor, dancing with other women.

As a man in silver body paint juggled in the background, my then-boyfriend yelled: 'If you walk away from me now, it's over!' And I remember thinking, *my mother didn't raise me to be the kind of person to ever give in to an ultimatum,* and I walked away, leaving him bathed in the fluorescent lights of Chiquito's.

That doesn't mean to say that I knew my own worth, or that I didn't go on to have tragic, bargain-basement expectations for most of the men in my life. I did, and made many mistakes, to the point where I fretted that I would never meet anyone, would never get married. While I didn't feel overt pressure to get married from my family while living in England – not in the way some of my other South Asian friends did – when I went back to India to visit family and friends, it felt more intense. Comments like 'when is it your turn?' ramped up, the higher I climbed into my twenties.

I didn't think it would happen for me, but when I turned twenty-eight, I met Rob Bell, a brilliant environmental journalist from New Zealand, who, with a shaved head and tattoos, didn't only look different to the men I'd dated before, but was like no other man I'd dated before. He was hard edges

SHE WANTED MORE

and softness, a ball of contradictions, from taking joy and delight in gardening to jumping up and down in a mosh pit at a punk gig. He was unbelievably clever and curious about the world and everything to do with nature, but he shut down when it came to his own issues (especially around the depression that had plagued him from a young age), believing he could solve them himself.

I've written about Rob and me extensively elsewhere, so I won't delve too much into our relationship, but in the first few months it moved with a fast undercurrent that carried us through deeper waters of wanting to get married and have children. When we lay next to each other in bed reading, I would sometimes look at him and feel the depth of that love. It felt limitless. I didn't have to worry about Rob's intensity of feeling, because I *felt* it. I never doubted how much he loved me, and I still don't.

On our wedding day, the first and strongest emotion I felt was peace; the second was happiness. To an extent, it was because I was marrying the love of my life, but there was also a sense of completion. That I had finally done the thing everyone had told me was so important. We settled into married life, and because I was only thirty at the time, there didn't seem to be any urgency about trying for kids. Besides, Rob appeared to be going through a depressive spell, and it felt more important to focus on his health.

A couple of years later, our entire world cracked apart. Rob wasn't only dealing with the depression he'd told me about at the start of our relationship, but he also confessed to being addicted to heroin. That in fact, around the time of our wedding, he'd been trying to withdraw from it. This made everything feel like a lie, and it broke open everything I thought I knew about the world, which was:

- Getting married was supposed to protect me from terrible things.
- Having a spouse meant I would be taken care of – and now I was the one caring.
- Our marriage was meant to be a 'happy ever after', but I didn't know if we would get through this.

During the two years that I helped Rob with his recovery, I learned that life was not fair and that some people get dealt a hard, tough hand. Everything doesn't happen for a reason. Society will lead you to the altar, insisting marriage is what you want, and then it will offer no support when things do not go smoothly. In fact, because of the interminable pressure to keep up appearances and pretend everything is fine, you will have to quietly digest your upset. And when you finally get the chance to scream it all out, as I did on the M4 while driving to a work event the day after my husband was admitted to a psychiatric hospital in 2014, you might not ever stop.

When the things that define you in society's eyes no longer exist – what does that make you? When I asked Betty, she said: 'I had never wondered who I was until 1987. Suddenly the three men in my life (my father, first husband and second husband), who had guided me up to that point, died within three months of one another. And I didn't know who I was. I was always whoever they thought I was.'

SHE WANTED MORE

You do not need the death of loved ones to push this message through. Instead, you can use the sharpening of time to figure out who you are. Who you've been. Who you want to be.

When Rob died in 2015 by suicide, I learned the hardest lesson of all. The people you think will be around forever, will not. Love is inherently loss – the fragility is what makes it beautiful – and nothing lasts forever. Not a house, not a job, not a long life, not safety – not even that grudge you're holding on to. So when I started to rebuild my life, I had to make space for the new things I wanted to invite in, by letting a few things go. I made a list of everything that I had believed was a truth, but in fact was not.

The list of lies I had believed until I turned forty (with a caveat that some of these were dismantled in my mid-thirties)

1) Men are allowed to build muscle; women are not
2) The goal for a woman is to be her slimmest self and to not look old
3) If you have brown skin, men will not find you attractive if it is *too* dark
4) If you put on weight, it means you have no self-control and no one will love you
5) If you want to lose weight, you have to take up running
6) If you have grey hair, you should dye it because otherwise you will look old
7) No one will want to fuck you if you look old
8) Menopause means the end of life as you know it, and

no one takes menopausal women seriously because of their hormones
9) Getting old means losing your strength, your cognitive abilities, diminishing
10) You must get married and have children in order to have a good life
11) If you have these things, you will be protected from sadness and loneliness
12) Being single means being lonely
13) Being with a partner means that I won't be lonely
14) Men take out the bins, do things with the car, know about plumbing, etc.
15) Men are in control of their finances and know more about money than women
16) Men automatically know how to fight even if they have never learned to fight
17) I look like a troll beast without makeup
18) Men are transparent and straightforward, and simple in their needs
19) I look better with long hair because it's more feminine
20) Getting older means the end of things in terms of physical capability
21) Someone who has kids and is married has somehow figured out how to do life in a way that I cannot
22) Men travel solo – it's too dangerous for women
23) Chastity is valued in women and the more partners you sleep with, the less respect you will get
24) Men care about fucking; women care about romance

25) It's the natural order of things that men are breadwinners

One of the most powerful learnings from being with Rob, and then his death, was that what I believed to be an innate truth about men was actually a lie told to women *and* men. The idea that men aren't emotional – that they don't feel deeply, that they don't experience things like loneliness, that they don't need softness and to be held, or they are simple in their thoughts – is one that damages us all. Although we live in a time of radicalisation of some boys and men who believe women are the reason for their misery, I remain optimistic that there are men who are trying to subvert this narrative.

They have their own weeding to do, especially because boys are still being told how to do masculinity according to a narrow framework, in order to be accepted by their peers. When they become adults, a lot of problems are caused by the way in which they perceive themselves falling short of this. While women bear a lot of the brunt of it, we cannot fix this for them and we cannot show them what to do – the catch-22 of patriarchy means that our voices don't have as much value to them, therefore they must engineer this change themselves. I want boys and men to be free to pursue everything that is perceived as an antonym to present-day masculinity – softness, conversation, vulnerability, fluidity – because that will positively impact us as well.

I don't believe that the assigned values we have around masculinity and femininity are inherent within us. Boys and girls tend to be given different types of messaging as they grow up, and these can impact the way our brains develop. Several studies show that when we are babies, girls tend to pick up linguistic and emotional skills faster because mothers talk to girl babies more than they talk to boy babies, while boy babies are praised more for their physical attributes such as crawling.[8] Consider that there is no gender gap between boys and girls when it comes to maths at pre-school, but a gap develops over time as self-expectations, shaped by the world, come into play.[9]

This belief, therefore, that women care more about marriage or even monogamy, feels like an implanted idea. So much of my life was built on believing that I needed a man by my side to achieve a sense of fullness because that is what I was told. When I think of the number of men I wasted time on, trying to achieve this, it is hard to know where to put that fury.

* * *

Other lies that are important to unravel: finances. We'll examine this further in the chapters about marriage and divorce, and in the final chapter, but there is a worrying rise in the number of younger women portraying 'getting men to pay for things' as a life hack. This is often framed as an easier solution to the economic grind than struggling to earn your own living at a time when salaries are shrinking. But the reality is that it is a return to a time when a woman's position was precarious because of her dependence on a man, underpinned by the legal system. Think about all the period dramas you've watched where women must dance around the archaic system of male inheritance. It feels like fiction because brave women over the course of history tirelessly protested and campaigned to make your reality a different one. Any encouragement to return to a time where 'a man is a financial plan' is therefore misguided.

See also: reframing the conversation around strength. After Rob died, I went on an unexpected journey which led me to competitive weightlifting. It started because I couldn't physically lift things around the house, and I hired a personal trainer to show me how to get strong. When I got stronger, I discovered it made me feel much more independent and capable. I didn't have to ask my dad to come over to help me move a bookcase because I could carry it myself. That made me realise the truth behind the 'telling women they had to be as small as possible' lie. Because if you keep women mad and weak with hunger, they *have* to keep men around to do the things they can't.

When I consider that, at the start of my weightlifting journey, I almost didn't want to lift heavier weights because it required me to build muscle and I worried about looking 'bulky', I have to almost admire the sophistication of the self-sabotage. And so, with all these things, I had to get real about what a system of oppression actually looked like, and question *why* women were made to believe certain things about ourselves.

Take, for instance, the belief that women should be as petite and small as possible. Not only does this make women physically easier to control (and the patriarchy loves that shit), telling women that lifting weights and developing muscle is for men prevents us from accessing strength training. This kind of training helps to build strong bones and helps to prevent osteoporosis (or brittle bone disease), which affects exponentially more women than men. Given that broken bones are 20% more fatal for elderly women than elderly men, this has a serious impact on our survival.[10]

When it comes to compiling your own list of lies, a helpful guideline is to look at things you believed were different about girls/women, versus boys/men. I personally believe that a fixed ideology around gender is harmful to everyone because it groups certain traits and behaviours and assigns them to masculinity or femininity. It harms the heterosexuals who live their lives within restrictive, self-imposed boundaries, and it harms everyone on the LGBTQ+ spectrum who may feel they have to hide or perform masculine or feminine traits in order to survive in certain spaces, or be penalised, abused and killed if they don't.

None of us benefit in a world where the rules about who we are, and how we should be, are so black and white.

Unravelling these lies doesn't mean rejecting life choices such as marriage and children (both can be incredibly rewarding); it just means thinking about what you're choosing and why you're choosing it. Some women want to stay at home with their children, while others do not. Some want to be with the same partner until death, and some want to love and have sex with many different people over the course of their lives. Some women want to alter their appearance as they age, and some women do not.

The most important thing is working out what comes

from within, and what has been told to us by an unknown authority. Then, when you identify a lie that no longer serves you, feeling a sense of courage and conviction in doing whatever you need to do to confront it and remove it from your life. For me, that ranged from things as nebulous as having the courage to say 'no' without feeling like a terrible person, to pursuing specific activities that had previously been labelled as masculine and therefore not open to a little South Asian woman like me.

On Substack, which is home to so many powerful female voices writing about the second and third act of our lives, I read a post by Ashley Kelsch, who runs a newsletter called *Unfucking Midlife*.

'You're not having a breakdown. You're having a breakthrough,' she wrote in one article, which hooked my attention. Based in Texas, she was married to a man twenty years older than her, who she had two children with. I asked her about why she decided to focus on womanhood and getting older.

'Equal parts courage and naivety enabled me to leave my marriage, become a single mother, and open a lingerie and wellness shop,' she told me. 'But I was still just young enough to confuse bold moves for clarity. I hadn't yet paused to examine what values were truly mine, versus the ones I'd been socialised and conditioned to accept. So, even after blowing up my life in all the "right" ways, I kept finding myself at the same crossroads of "crises" asking: *Why isn't this working? Why do I still feel this way? Everyone else seems to have it figured out – what's wrong with me?*

'Now, in my mid-forties, I see it differently. And frankly,

I won't waste time spinning out in a so-called crisis. I know from experience that these moments are signals – signs that I need to look closely at my life and the choices I've made. They're telling me I'm out of alignment with where I'm meant to be going.'

Hormones can help force this change through by helping us give fewer shits about the consequences, but it can't do everything. It cannot dig up the weeds in our garden. Whatever rootlessness you are feeling, whatever uncertainty or lack of trust you have in your own decision-making – this was not something you gave away. It was something that was ripped out and replaced with things that were never designed to make you flourish and grow.

That is going to have to come from a place deep inside us, and we are going to have to change how we think, radically. As Bianca said, in the 'She Wanted More' survey: 'My wish for other women is to stop apologising for ourselves and making ourselves small to fit in. Make noise, stand tall and just be.'

It is your life, and your truth. It is time to take back control of your own mind, your basic rights as a human being, the belief in yourself, that you are a creature of this planet with every right to exist, to love, to thrive and feel nothing but life force and warmth and safety.

Take back every ounce of that power – and burn all the weeds to the ground.

CHAPTER THREE

HARNESSING POWER, ANGER AND CHANGE

If I could rebuild my life after losing Rob, I could do anything. I knew that in my bones.

For anyone who doubts their ability to be brave and to engineer change, anchor this uncertainty to a moment of truth when you did something you never thought you could do. Or when something changed even though you were convinced it wouldn't.

Beyond Rob, the pandemic played a massive part in my renegotiation around the ageing narrative, and actively pursuing the things that made me feel powerful and good. Covid was fucking awful but it was a truth-teller. The shutting down of our world was a reminder that we have control over very little, that things are not promised to us just because we followed all the steps on the heteronormative flowchart to Neverending Happiness, and that perception is everything.

Why should thirty feel different to twenty-nine, or

thirty-one? If the only power a number wields is the value we assign it, then surely removing these values will free us from unnecessary pain and pressure? If I hadn't been locked inside my own house with nothing but time, I don't know that I would have given it much thought. But I was forced to consider things such as purpose, power and meaning.

When we emerged out of lockdown in 2021, I knew I had been feeling stuck for the last couple years, but I didn't know how much, until I decided to keep an open mind and try new things. One of those was dabbling in non-monogamy. I dated a man who was in an open marriage – his wife also had another partner. While I'm not sure I would ever try it again – if anything because the admin involved will break even an executive personality type on the Myers–Briggs scale – it led me to a community which was mind-expanding in terms of seeing how differently life could be arranged.

It forced me to confront how small I had made my world in an attempt to control things during the early grief years, especially because the person I'd dated had such an exuberant, spontaneous love of life. Over the years, I'd got into a bad habit of cancelling social plans. *I probably won't like that*, I told myself, and stayed at home. After dating (and breaking up with) Mr Spontaneous, I gave myself permission to leave whenever I wanted (whether it was a party, a date or a work event), and I slowly began to say yes to things. This approach changed my life and showed that I might just have a good time even when I'm being an Eeyore about it.

Perhaps the most powerful change was the physical rebuild I had to undertake after Covid robbed me of my strength overnight. As a competitive powerlifter, I had gone from someone who was able to lift 120kg to a mere 20kg barbell – and even that was impossible for several months. When I realised my body had shrugged off Long Covid, it was deeply confronting to start lifting again because I was no longer in my thirties. I had been told my whole life that getting older meant getting weaker – what if I wasn't as strong? What if being in my forties was the beginning of the end?

When I spoke to my coach and friend Jack about the paranoia around ageing and getting weaker, he said that, while you need more protein and rest as you get older, there is no physiological reason why you can't keep getting stronger. You might not be competing in the Olympics or be able to recover as quickly as people in their twenties, but the idea that getting older automatically defaults to frailty is simply not true.

I got back on the platform a year later, the day before my forty-first birthday. In a draughty Surrey gym, drinking coffee to keep warm, I realised this wasn't just about reclaiming my strength; it was about rewriting what I believed about my future.

A powerlifting competition is where you do three attempts of three lifts – squat, bench and deadlift – in front of a judge, but it isn't really about the day itself. You want to hit the numbers you've set for yourself, prove that you can perform under pressure, but really the work begins weeks and months before that. You have to train steadily and consistently, and over time, I watched in disbelief as my strength started to come back. A part of me had believed that I might never access it again, and had that been the case, I would have made my peace with it. But its return felt more precious, having known its loss.

Before the pandemic, and before turning forty, I had tried to deadlift 125kg in a competition but failed. While I had (just about) managed to get the bar up, my technique was terrible, and the judges rightly failed the lift. In the aftermath of everything, I stood in front of the bar again – 125kg – with a sea of people in front of me, including my friends and family.

My hands gripped the bar, the calluses resting against the ridges. As I pulled the bar all the way up, I felt that flood of power. Easier than last time, higher stakes this time. And as the white lights came on, and the judge gave me a thumbs up to say it had passed, I realised something.

Even if I hadn't got that bar all the way up, even if I hadn't so much as shifted it off the ground, it dawned on me that I was a woman in my forties, dressed in a singlet that left nothing to the imagination, lifting heavy weights in front of a crowd. And while that might sound like the stuff of nightmares to someone else, to me it was the start of changing the story. Of being a woman, of getting older, of realising something about power and where it truly resides. Not in anyone else but me.

Your life may be determined by circumstance, or the choices you've made in the past. While that claiming of power looks different for every one of us – know that it has always belonged to you.

* * *

When I was younger, ageing did not feel like power.

My thirties were not like most people's, primarily because

my husband died when I was thirty-four, but it would have been a cathartic decade regardless. None of the wisdom I was told to expect arrived during my early thirties. My career still felt uncertain and precarious, and I still cared too much about what other people thought and prioritised their needs. By the time I reached thirty-nine, I thought I should be a grown-up, but I didn't feel like one. The next stage of life – whatever that was supposed to look like – terrified me, and the waterfall of my stream of consciousness around ageing was:

Backache no sex menopause hot flushes no desire grey hair tired frail loss of control illness weight gain loss darkening sadness giving up

I'm not unusual in this. When I ran the 'She Wanted More' survey, the words that positively resonated around getting older included *freedom, contentment, peacefulness* and *the option to do what you want*. But there were also negative associations, such as *feeling fearful and scared*. Some of the most common worries were *fading away, loss of mobility, being alone, being overlooked*, and *not being able to retire*.

When my fortieth birthday arrived at the end of 2020, it surprisingly revealed something I might not have valued had the world not shut down. My parents' house was not where I had planned to be celebrating, back when I was debating whether to throw a party or get drunk on a beach. But in light of all that had happened that year, being in the same space with my loved ones, my sister and then six-year-old niece bundling into my room to hug and kiss me in the morning, was exactly where I wanted to be. *I am safe, and I am loved*, I thought, and the entirety of my world was within four walls.

For some of us, the pandemic deepened our relationships with our partners and children, prompting a re-evaluation of priorities once the world opened up again. For others, it showed the inequities even more starkly, especially around who continued to do more domestic labour or carry the emotional load in the relationship. For people like me, who spent most of it single and alone, it reassured us about our ability to continue even when things got tough. I missed Rob, but I didn't long to be in a relationship. I didn't sit there alone on my sofa and think, *this would be better with a man*. Meanwhile for others it showed up the deep loneliness they had been grappling with beforehand but had distracted themselves from, with work and friends.

Grief had turned me into a control freak, and Covid humbled me. I couldn't keep my loved ones safe in the face of a global pandemic, and it showed up my sense of control for what it was: an illusion. I hadn't noticed the extent to which fear and worry had been strangling my life, until I decided to let them go. As oxygen flooded in, life expanded and bloomed because of it. Speaking to the author and broadcaster Pandora Sykes for her newsletter *Books and Bits*, the author, philosopher and *Guardian* columnist Oliver Burkeman said: 'What we find is that the more we exert that control, the less vibrancy there is. Life actually becomes less, as the things that make life worth living get squeezed out. You need, in some sense, to be surprised by the world, or by another person. There's nothing vibrant in a relationship where you know exactly what the other person is going to do at all times.'

SHE WANTED MORE

The pandemic was the perfect opportunity for people to reset because so many different structures and dynamics were in flux, from gender roles to workplace culture, but it is possible to replicate that change *if* you are brave enough to say goodbye to a certain aspect of safety.

It reminded me of something Ashley Kelsch wrote: 'The most disruptive act in midlife isn't leaving your job or relationship – it's leaving behind the version of yourself that you created in order to survive.'

That one sentence was an arrow threading all my disparate thoughts together. It was shot in an arc towards a horizon. A horizon that didn't involve reclaiming my youth or trying to stop time, but one that glimmered with the possibility of what could be if I shrugged off what no longer served me.

* * *

When I turned forty, I wrote and spoke a lot about the empowering experience of it, but it still felt paradoxical. On the one hand, I had discovered a new well of confidence that felt deeper than anything that had come before. On the other, it was like walking on ice, not knowing which parts were thinnest, until I stepped through and cold fear flooded my body. I didn't know if I was making the right decisions because, like a lot of women, my only reference points for being this age were based on the past and the ideas held by my mother's generation.

I feel like I know everything and nothing. This sense of duality is such a common trait among women who are older than Gen Z – caught between the sense of what we should be doing, and what we want to do; between obligation and desire; between knowing more than we have ever known before, and still not knowing what the future holds for us.

When you're trying to make sense of your life and what you want from it, a few things can get in the way. The first is a sense of toxic positivity. Some people say things like: *Age is nothing but a number! Who cares? Ageing is a privilege – just be happy!* Ageing *is* a privilege, but that doesn't help when you are trying to find meaning and purpose in a world that has set ideas about what that age means for you. Whenever I write about dating and being in my forties, some mouth-breather writes in the comments: 'Women over 40 are EXPIRED.' I follow influencers in their fifties and sixties on social media who are regularly told they are behaving or dressing in a way that is 'embarrassing' because of their age, and not just by men.

If age was just a number, we wouldn't talk about it endlessly or have a billion-dollar industry dedicated to making us look younger. You cannot just hope that a positive attitude will change the ageism in our society – it requires us to be visible, doing active work to challenge the beliefs around what getting older means, and for institutions to change how they view and treat people past a certain age.

You can know that ageing is a privilege and still find it hard. You can tell yourself not to care about what people think, and still find that your mind boomerangs towards caring quite a bit. You are made to fear the future even though it is a time of liberation, because your uncertainty makes you easier to control.

SHE WANTED MORE

It strikes me that the conversation around ageing, and feeling galvanised in our lives, has some strong parallels with diet culture and the body confidence movement.

Standing in front of a mirror saying you love yourself, while trying to live in the constant reality of a fatphobic society, is probably not going to lead to actual self-acceptance. What tends to work better is deconstructing where that story began, identifying who was horrible to us about our bodies when we were younger, taking small steps to create a big change over time, and repairing our relationship with food. It is hard work, it is multi-faceted, and it also feels true about getting older.

You are told that as you get older, you give fewer fucks about everything, from ageing to people-pleasing, and that it can be liberating! Life-changing! But it's okay to give a few fucks.

As I get older, I feel I'm approaching a closer approximation to figuring out what I want to detach from, and what I want to run towards.

'I know there's a lot of "I no longer give a fuck" kind of talk around the freedom that middle age brings,' Hollie McNish said, 'and I get it, but I don't love that framing. I think we give a fuck about so, so much, just not the shite we've been told to focus on for years.'

The concept of care is one we'll expand on, but part of this current shift for women is around the twin rejection of: 1) caring solely based on gender, for instance, assuming you care about certain things or will provide care just because you are a woman; and 2) being expected to endlessly care and provide service to your loved ones until your final breath.

On TikTok, a viral movement of women in their forties and fifties exists called the 'We Do Not Care Club' (WDNC), started by Melani Sanders, a 46-year-old American woman who gained a million followers after posting a list of things that peri-menopausal women no longer give a shit about. Every day, women post videos applying to open their own 'chapter' of WDNC in their hometown – all over the world. A lot of it is based on things that people (including loved ones) just expect them to do that they are no longer doing, and things they aren't bothering with around their appearance.

Sanders starts every video with 'announcements' from her members stating things they no longer care about, and favourites include being asked to pick up groceries. 'Everybody else in this house drove past the same store,' she reads out loud in one video. 'Don't ask us why we didn't get it. Ask yourself why you didn't get it.' One of my favourites was a woman saying that she sat on the floor and ate straight out of her fridge because a) it cooled her down and b) she didn't want to do any washing up.

Women still give a fuck about a lot of things. Gender equality, political injustice, women's health and rights. The safety and happiness of their loved ones. They no longer want to give a fuck about the things that men don't have to give a fuck about, because there's always been a woman to give a fuck about it. One of my side hustles is public speaking, and in corporations it's the women who tend to be the organisers of inhouse events and the ones who scurry around serving food and water, while the expectation for the men is that they *show*

SHE WANTED MORE

up on time if at all. I don't think these women want to give a fuck about organising the events but they know that if they don't, it won't end up happening.

In their personal lives, see also: buying presents, filling the fridge, managing joint calendars, making sure laundry is done, being the person who always makes the bookings, ironing, going to baby showers, hen dos, performing friendship, the group chat, meal prep, waiting for people who are permanently late, wearing heels, wearing underwired bras, wearing thongs, wearing makeup, celebrities not eating carbs on the day they have to wear a tight-fitting dress while their male counterpart wears a t-shirt on the red carpet.

'A lot of women spend the first half of their lives in service to others,' Ashley said. 'Their roles – mother, partner, caregiver, employee – come first. Their own needs, dreams and identities come second, if at all. At some point, whether it's triggered by burnout, a hormonal shift, the realisation that time is finite, or just being sick and tired of being sick and tired, something shifts.

'They start to want more. Not more to do – but more of themselves. More truth. More time. More agency. There's this deep knowing that life is happening now, and if they're going to live it fully, it has to look and feel different than it has before.'

You wanting more from your life doesn't mean caring less. It means caring about different things, and it means that other people need to care *more*. And it's okay to be angry about it when they don't. When they call you selfish, use it. Use that as a moment to remind yourself that a woman is expected to give and give and give and even when her health suffers, even when the light has gone out of her eyes, it is never enough. It's okay to use that anger to push through to what you need because if you don't, you will get eaten up by your rage.

I spoke to psychotherapist Jennifer Cox, co-host of the *Women Are Mad* podcast, about this. Jen wrote a book called *Women Are Angry*, which was part of the zeitgeist around women's anger. 'The factor which unites women who *have* been able to find more peace and contentment,' she said, 'is being able to acknowledge and healthily discharge their rage and inherent sense of injustice. While we're still so far from anything which feels genuinely equitable in the world, we need to try to establish a sort of inner conveyor belt which helps us healthily process more negative emotions.'

Anger, change, fear – these are big topics, but I want to reassure anyone wondering whether they have to blow their life up, that I am definitely *not* suggesting you need to do that. However, the reason why connecting with anger, and with what irritates you, is important, is because it is a warning bell being rung. It is telling you that someone is taking too much or you are giving too much. But it is also fuel. When you are trying to take your power back from people, anger is the kinetic force that will allow you to shed your doubts and do that with clarity and purpose.

* * *

I wanted to sense-check some of the things we'll be exploring in the book, and for that I needed Sam Baker, former editor of *Red* magazine, author, founder of *The Shift* podcast that has featured many erudite and accomplished women, from Miranda July to Dame Sheila Hancock. Sam is also one of the pioneers in the movement to get people talking about life for women over forty.

As we sipped our tea, she said, 'Gen X were the first "have it all" generation. And we were the ones that discovered that having it all meant doing it all.' Back in the fifties, she said, university was something that privileged white middle-class American women attended in order to find a husband, but for Sam's generation it wasn't. Women were there to get an education. But alongside that, the goals of marriage and kids hadn't gone away – they were meant to exist alongside a working life. It was a trap to sell women more freedom and conceal that it was just more labour – creating the impossible expectation to do all of it brilliantly.

'It's inevitable,' she says, 'this sense of questioning: what am I? You get to this point, whether that's after your children have left home or when you near the end of your working life, where you think: Well, I'm not just going to go quietly. So what am I for? And I do think that's why a lot of women, maybe slightly older than me, maybe more retirement age, are like, "Okay, what next? What's my purpose now?"'

For millennials, the conflict around purpose is similar but different. As is the case with every generation that builds on the learnings of others, they have a better grasp of issues concerning their mental wellbeing, whether that's workplace environment or life balance. They were the first generation to grow up with the internet and have mobile phones, and that was a huge step change technologically, because of the information they were able to access. Their diversity of network, if we factor in social media, was vastly bigger than the kind Gen X would have been able to tap into at their age.

That doesn't mean they are without their struggles though. Although they are tipped to be 'the richest generation' once they inherit, until that happens, they are currently not doing at all well financially.[11] Gen Z and younger millennials are increasingly struggling with a large debt burden incurred by student loans and the cost of living, according to the Fairness Foundation. Even the concept of money has changed – my generation worked so hard in our twenties, often to the detriment of our health, because we thought wealth was the most important thing, while the younger generation is questioning whether it is worth sacrificing your mental wellbeing for. Amy Poehler said in her podcast *Good Hang*: 'Boomers are all about money. Gen X is like: is it all about the money? Millennials are like: where is the money? Gen Z is like: what is money?'

Money is important to mention because of how much it impacts choices and freedom for women. If we are talking about empowerment and liberation, it must be acknowledged that these may feel secondary in the day-to-day life of a woman who needs to work several jobs to afford childcare and food. When I asked Sam about it, she agreed that while it's great that the idea of change is being championed for forty-plus women, some women, who are less confident and less privileged, may not feel they can access it. Especially when it is couched as 'reinvention'.

If you are mostly content with your life – and over half

the people who took the 'She Wanted More' survey reported feeling contented – you may find the representations of older women online and onscreen polarising. They are usually sexy, thin and rich.

'Like all of a sudden you have to be amazing and dynamic at fifty,' Sam said. 'Someone said to me, *I'm knackered*. And we were initially talking about J Lo and Shakira and the pressure to still be hot. I try to be careful not to make the women who feel stuck, and scared, feel worse. They have been made to feel bad their whole lives because they're not thin enough, they're not fit enough, they're not successful, and all those "enoughs". Most people I know who are happy are people with much smaller lives.'

I asked author, psychologist and behavioural change expert Shahroo Izadi about it, and she said: 'I think the word reinvention can feel like a betrayal – especially for those of us who have spent decades trying to feel acceptable and lovable as we are. By forty, many of us are proud of our values and feel more intentional than ever about how we live. So the idea that we now need to reinvent ourselves – as if there's still some unseen audience we need to win over – can feel exhausting or even insulting.'

Growth, she says, is a better way of looking at it. 'It is a far more sustainable and compassionate idea than reinvention. Growth feels inwardly inspired. Reinvention often feels outwardly driven, as if we still need to perform or transform for someone else's approval. The goal isn't to become someone new. It's to become more yourself – to keep returning to who you were before the world told you who you needed to be.'

Looking outward to what is already visible is never going to be a perfect solution. Social media is a messy part of that. On the one hand it roadmaps more diverse ways of existing, which wouldn't be possible if we just stuck to our own social circles. But at the same time, we get overwhelmed by the constant need to decide what is the right or wrong thing to do. We look at how other people are arranging their lives and wonder if we should be doing the same. Or feel terrible because we don't measure up. And then we argue about the right way to do it. Have cosmetic work, don't have it. Take HRT, don't take it.

'What worries me,' said Sam Baker, 'is that we wanted visibility, and now we've got the pressure and the comparison that comes with visibility. It sets a different benchmark, and it's still impossible to reach.'

There is never going to be one right way to change – even if people tell you that there is. I do want women to want more for themselves and I also don't want them to feel as if they are failing, or aren't 'cool enough' because they aren't changing their lives in big ways. (A woman sent me a message to that effect, saying that she was married with kids, and had no desire to change her life – which was valid if somewhat unnecessary.) Even in a conversation about broadening choices for women, we have a tendency to create cliques around the types of choices and what we perceive they say about us. Traditional choices don't automatically equate to being backward-looking, and radical choices don't automatically equate to selfishness or immorality.

Debating what ageing means now, in the post-'having it

all' era, and charting the choices that women are making for ourselves, is necessary because of the nuance within those choices. It doesn't have to be the case that you blow your life up. Your definition of 'more' could be as gentle as asking yourself what you want to invite into your life. Who do you want to be right now? What do you want to do more of? And what kind of older woman do you want to be?

Sari Botton's words provided a lot of comfort while I was pondering this. 'The older I get the more I discover that while certain physiological challenges of aging are undeniable, there are so many ways in which we become *more* later in life, not less,' she said. 'We grow wiser, more secure, more compassionate, more true to who we really are. Those things are huge, and they make getting older a joy.'

Once we are able to claim back our energy from things that no longer serve us, asking what gives us joy, what makes us feel like the most full, peaceful version of ourselves is a good compass as we navigate the next few chapters, steering through a core topic that occupies so much of our waking thoughts: relationships, marriage, dating, divorce and being single.

CHAPTER FOUR

MARRIAGE AND LONG-TERM RELATIONSHIPS: THE GOOD, THE BAD AND THE TRUTHFUL

A rite of passage in England at the age of sixteen was to get a work placement as part of your schooling. I knew I wanted to be a journalist but I also knew it would be hard to get experience, especially as the Kent suburbs weren't exactly a hotbed of reporting. I kept my hopes low, until a teacher told me that a placement at the *Kent Messenger* was mine, and I SCREAMED with excitement.

That enthusiasm continued until my first day, when I was assigned to a chain-smoking sixty-year-old woman named Doris who organised the classifieds. She asked me to cut out the ads that had run in previous editions, and when I suspiciously asked what she was going to do with them because this felt like a task one would assign to distract a small child, she winked and said: 'It's a secret'. A reporter named Darren took pity on me, perhaps concerned that Doris's plumes of smoke might stunt my already scrawny body, and asked me to help him research a story.

A Dartford-based centenarian named Ellen was turning 101, and we were tasked with finding out the secret of her longevity. 'People love that shit,' Darren said. It reminded me of Adrian Mole's elderly friend Bert Baxter being interviewed about his love of beetroot and Woodbine cigars. Ellen was quite reticent with her answers, so I suggested that we ask what advice she had for younger people instead. 'You know, like what she'd do differently,' I explained.

'No one is interested in that,' said Darren dismissively. 'They want to know that Ellen ate bacon sandwiches every day and still managed to live a long life.'

When I next got the chance to talk to a centenarian almost thirty years later, the former US Park Ranger Betty Reid Soskin, I didn't waste her time asking what sandwiches she ate. I wanted to ask her about being part of the civil rights movement in the 1960s, and how she worked towards the development of a park to honour women who helped on the home front in the Second World War. I wanted to ask her about the breakdown she suffered in her forties.

In a PBS interview, when she was asked what advice she might have for herself as a younger woman, her words took me by surprise: 'My advice would be to never marry,' she said. Adding: 'I could've done all the things I've done in my life, without a man.'

This is a woman who has done it all according to society's playbook, and more than what was asked. And while people almost always feel attacked for their choices whenever marriage is critiqued, the sentiment here isn't anti-marriage, or to say that marriage is bad. It's to wake women up around marriage. To reset the factory settings. To actively choose it, rather than feeling it's something you should do, or must do, and realise certain truths before entering into it. To understand that marriage shouldn't be a diminishing but an amplification of what exists between the two of you, and that compromise doesn't mean giving up who you *are*. And whether you are in a marriage or a long-term partnership, to remember that you have choices. Not necessarily to exit it, but to evolve and grow *with* your partner, not *in spite of them*.

According to Rachael Lennon, who wrote *Wedded Wife: A Feminist History of Marriage*, 'generations of women in the past found that their only means of accessing sex and parenthood, a household and opportunities to contribute to society, was as a married woman'.

Depending on geography, culture and religion, for some women, this is still true. But for some of us, it is not. We do have choices, and it's important to know what they are.

In this chapter, while a lot of what I posit is relevant for long-term relationships, it is heavily weighted towards addressing marriage. Although long-term partnerships also have financial complications when assets are combined, marriage is a different kind of legal contract that further complicates things. We will also look at how women have positively renegotiated and evolved their marriages, which I feel will be helpful to people who feel stuck. Finally, I want to underline the seriousness of what marriage is, beyond the shiny lure of a wedding.

In the survey I ran, 67% of women were married to a man, and 33% of those also had children. In total, 70% of these women said they were happy in their marriages, despite the fact that nearly half of them do more domestic labour than their husbands. In terms of a living situation, 59% of them said they would still choose to live with their partner, and 33% would prefer a hybrid situation of living together sometimes but not full-time. Only 8% said they would prefer to live separately.

All of this indicates that when it comes to marriage, there is complexity around what we want and what we compromise around. While we can agree that society conditions women to want marriage more (because we are told that our chief marker of success is domestic, while for men it is economic), the reasons we might want it are varied. It could be anything from seeking a sense of safety and belonging with another person, to wanting to share life with someone else, to having and raising children with someone.

When I was younger, there was so much focus on the status of being married, but much less talking about what it actually entailed. The only time I started to get advice on the realities of being married was when I opened our wedding cards, after Rob and I had signed our lives away to each other. Everything before that was laser focused on a) getting a man to agree to marriage (and there was a pervasive sense that he might need convincing, as if you were asking for something he might not want) and b) the wedding day.

SHE WANTED MORE

For women, in particular, there is so much emphasis on the wedding day and how it's FINALLY YOUR SPECIAL DAY! It is dangled like a reward for being able to get all the things you want. And we have to ask ourselves why. Why do I need a wedding day to get what I want? To have the attention I deserve, to feel seen? Why is the wedding day not pushed in the same way to men? Why are we not taught what equality in a marriage looks like? And why are we taught that our centre of gravity, the thing that gives us purpose and meaning, is our status as it relates to a man? And why are we not taught that we can arrange our relationships differently to each other and without shame?

It is there that I think we will find answers as to how to get more from marriage, and for some of us to figure out if it is right for us at all. Let's get into it.

* * *

Here's what I think I know about marriage – especially marriage to a heterosexual man. I know that the bond between Rob and I deepened once we became husband and wife. It wasn't just a piece of paper. It was a promise to each other, an intention to be each other's families, to choose each other. It was different to being in a long-term relationship, and that isn't to say it was more valid but it held power because we *gave* it power.

Yuval Noah Harari wrote in his book *Sapiens* that the cognitive revolution, which happened 70,000 years ago, enabled us to believe in imagined realities – social constructs that allow us to co-operate. 'Two lawyers who have never met can nevertheless combine efforts to defend a complete stranger because they both believe in the existence of laws, justice, human rights – and the money paid out in fees,' he wrote. 'Yet none of these things exist outside the stories that people invent and tell one another. There are no gods in the universe, no nations, no money, no human rights, no laws and no justice outside the common imagination of human beings.'

Marriage initially existed as a contractual agreement to produce children, secure alliances and make money – the earliest record of it is apparently from Mesopotamian times almost 4,300 years ago. It has evolved to mean something else. While arranged marriages still exist, most marriage is now underpinned by the narrative of finding a soulmate thanks to the Romantic era of the eighteenth century, and it is positioned as the inevitable conclusion to falling in love with someone. Let's be clear, however: marriage has never been, and currently is not, an equitable contract between both partners because of the inequities facing women around domestic labour, equal pay and maternity leave.

Currently, the 'soulmate-to-marriage' pipeline is in crisis, and is in need of seismic change if marriage is to survive as a social construct. A report was published in 2024 that showed for the first time on record, marriage and civil partnership rates in the UK dropped below 50 per cent (in the US it is 60 per cent), and almost 90 per cent of the world's population lives in countries with declining marriage rates.[12] That might be partly due to financial reasons; another factor might be shifting gender roles.

If marriage was equitable for women, I don't think the

far right would be pushing 'traditional values' so hard. Old fears are being resurrected – the idea that women's worth is defined by their virtue (think about all the bro podcasts that refer to 'body count', aka the number of people a woman has had sex with). Also, the idea that women earn 'value' if they prioritise motherhood and marriage (and conversely if you don't have either, you're a dusty, godless crone with moths in your nether regions). These all seek to control women's behaviour and recentre men.

Tradwives are an excellent demonstration of how some women are co-opted by the far right to encourage other women to give up their autonomy. A tradwife is different from a homemaker, in that she is a woman who promotes and encourages a rejection of feminism, and a return to good old-fashioned 1950s gender roles where the woman in the household lives to serve her husband and children. She's not an equal (as a homemaker is) – she agrees to come second to her husband in every respect.

The tradwife indirectly makes life harder for women who legitimately choose to become homemakers because looking after a home is still a form of labour. Like any form of labour, it has a monetary value attached to it, but in the tradwife world, this labour is presented as something a woman likes to do simply because she is a woman. Although she has vehemently denied being a tradwife, one of the most famous figureheads of the movement is the model and influencer Nara Smith, who, with twelve million followers on TikTok, has portrayed the idea of tradwifing being a more serene, calm way of being. She'd record videos of her making things from scratch for her children while wearing elaborate outfits and talking in an ASMR whisper. Whether or not she intended it, it created a shorthand that this was a more beautiful, elevated way of being, and for women who were tired and ground down by the hustle of life, it was appealing.

When I first heard about tradwives, I thought it was satire. What woman would choose to give up the rights so many others had fought for? It was like a prisoner asking to go back into their cell – it didn't make sense. But, when we factor in the tough economy and how hard it is for women to survive in it, I can see why having someone else to steer the ship might seem attractive. It takes care of your financial woes and gives you a sense of purpose, even if that purpose is hand-scrubbing your husband's undies and whittling your own cereal from what were once your hopes and dreams.

'With the resurgence of the tradwife ideal,' said author and podcaster Candice Brathwaite, 'coupled with a tough economy, so much of the rhetoric I'm seeing is skewed towards the idea that being "chosen" is still the ultimate goal.

'It irks me no end. Married or not, ways in which I can "keep someone" just doesn't keep me up at night. A husband will stay or go. Who am I outside of that? I've learned that my marriage is best when I always keep myself and my desires at the forefront. This isn't to say that I'm unwilling to think of my husband, but when it comes to the woman, often so little is left for the self.'

Although women's rights are dire in some parts of the world, in other parts they have changed a lot in a very short space of time (when you compare this to other social evolutions in history), from issues like the right to vote, to financial agency and inclusion of different sexual identities. However, some of these things – especially independence and equally shared labour – are in direct contrast to how most marriages are arranged these days, with women still doing most of the domestic and emotional labour.

Every time I post about this on social media, I get a few defensive responses from women saying their husbands do an equal share of the work. But this isn't meant as an attack on men or the state of your relationship – only *you* can decide what feels fair, and rarely are things such as finances and labour perfectly equal because life doesn't neatly split into 50/50. However, some of us do have a skewed sense of how much our partners actually do. I thought Rob and I were equals because he cooked and did chores, but I still had to largely organise him. It forced me into the role of nag, and I *hated* having to be the one who always remembered and sorted things out. For me, partnership comes down to: do I trust you to take responsibility to get the basic things we need doing in our lives, without having to remind you or explain why they are important? And I have never been in a partnership like that.

If you're truly in a relationship where you feel your male partner does an equal share and where you don't have to organise him, you are the exception, not the rule. A 2019 UCL study of 8,500 different-sex couples found that only 7% of couples share housework equally,[13] while the Covid-19 pandemic showed that women had an increase in their workload compared to men, even when both parties were at home, according to the World Economic Forum.[14]

While men have got better at taking on more of the domestic work than their fathers, it is still viewed as less important than paid work. When a female friend debates the idea of quitting her job to become a full-time homemaker, I hesitate to be enthusiastic about it not because I don't value homemaking as a job, but because I doubt whether her male partner has truly done the deep, internal work to respect it as such. Furthermore, I don't want my friend to feel her worth being devalued simply because her partner is not evolved or educated enough in gender politics to reset what we've been told – that domestic labour is women's work and we should be doing it anyway.

Perhaps if there was a monetary value attached to domestic work, it might shift the perception of how much each person contributes. In 2021, there was a landmark divorce case in China, where a man was ordered to pay his wife for the housework she had done during their five-year-marriage. It was significant because, for the first time in China, it placed a value on all the unpaid work done at home, which has often been bundled together as 'women's work'.[15]

If a social construct exists because enough people say it does, and if the social contract that binds it is not equally beneficial to all the people who take part in it, why can we not change it so that it better suits us as individuals? Marriage can be great because it provides safety, companionship and someone to have children with (if that's what you want), but somehow most of us feel pressured to go along with a definition of it that isn't quite working for us. When I have spoken to older women who have found themselves single and living alone again, either through divorce or the death of a spouse, a common response – like Betty's – is that they have no wish to do it again. Or rather, they'd choose to do it differently.

When I interviewed the author and fashion influencer Lyn Slater, seventy-two, who wrote *How to Be Old*, she told me she had been with her partner Calvin for twenty-seven years. When they met, she was forty-five and had been divorced for five years. They met at a bookbinding course, and a blossoming friendship deepened into something romantic.

'From the start,' she said, 'we set ground rules for our relationship based on past experience and a good amount of self-awareness. Our relationship then and now has continued to be more practical than aspirational. Independence foremost (we keep financial affairs separate and jointly share all expenses) and only have a say (unless asked) in individual decisions that directly have an impact on the other. This has resulted in a healthy dependence when pragmatic and necessary.

'We take responsibility for our lifestyle choices, our duty of care towards each other and have legal documents that protect each of us because we are not legally married. We are clear with each other when we need help and when we do not. We unreservedly support each other's personal growth and creative expression. We are both seriously committed to lifelong learning. We work on understanding and valuing our differences; when they are complementary and when they can create conflict (learning to communicate without blame has been key). The lifestyle we have chosen has given us the joyful freedom of waking up every day knowing we are making a choice to be together, not because we must but because we want to.'

Lyn's wisdom got me thinking. Looking at marriage in its current iteration – is living with and being legally tied to a man worth the benefits it supposedly brings? For some women, it appears not. It's not about demonising men, but rather that these women no longer want to compromise on their preferences or do more labour, and that they are fine without them.

A 2025 study from the University of Alberta revealed that the gap in domestic labour began when a woman was around twenty-five and increased with age, especially when children were introduced.[16] And if this gap was not addressed or renegotiated, it could lead to deep resentment. Matthew Johnson, a relationship researcher and lead author on the study, said: 'If you're happy with the way things are going, that's great. But if not, you have to do something to change that pattern, and make a plan with your partner. It's important for couples to be intentional about how they organise these aspects of their life – because how those tasks are managed is likely to continue into the future.'

Therefore, when we think about the future of heterosexual marriage, it doesn't mean getting rid of it. (For queer people, in fact, retaining or legalising the right to get married is a very different conversation, because it is a proxy for acceptance of homosexuality and validation in the eyes of mainstream society. The far right is currently trying to strip this as a right, because, y'know – fascism.) Many people find marriage rewarding and an essential pillar of their contentment in life, despite that 2019 statistic that unmarried, childfree women are the happiest demographic. Incidentally, that was based on the findings of behavioural science professor Paul Dolan, who wrote *Happy Ever After: The Myth of the Perfect Life*, and we've subsequently found that married women tend to be happier than unmarried women *when* the marriage is good. When it's bad, it can affect their health in terrible ways, and over time, it is likely to adversely affect women more than men because of the accumulation of labour within the marriage.

Evolution and renegotiation should be the norm in any type of relationship. Over the years, I have seen so many women put up with men who clearly do not want the same things as them, who have stayed in relationships that are deeply unfulfilling, to fulfil the marriage narrative they've been told to want. Women should know that it's okay to want more from their marriages; and that doesn't necessarily mean doing more, but rather doing things differently.

Margaret Murphy, seventy-one, appeared on the BBC and in *The Guardian* talking about her decision to leave her husband and children back in Australia, and move to London at the age of fifty-six. She'd spent thirty years as a homemaker and after her mother died, saw this as a time to do something for herself. She got her first full-time job at the age of sixty as an education officer. The twist is that she is still happily married to Peter, and they see each other on visits, but what started as an initial itch to travel and see a bit of the world evolved into something different.

Consider that if marriage is a construct, we can have a say in its architecture. The biggest things holding people back from changing things are either convention, or competing with others around decisions like where you go on holiday, the size of your house, or where your kids go to school. Who gives a fuck what your friends are doing or what the parents at the school gate say? Let's go a step further – take your kids out of the equation and, for a moment, look at the foundation of your marriage. What works well? What do you like about your partner? Can you see yourself spending the next decade with things being exactly as they are now? What could change *right now* if you didn't feel so constrained by social norms?

Having these conversations should be a normal part of the engagement process, and yet we aren't educated or taught much about their importance. Which strikes me as bizarre, because – apart from having children – legally binding yourself to another person is the biggest undertaking you can make. Especially if you are a woman. It changes every aspect of your life, determines the choices you make, and the amount of freedom you have.

* * *

There is so much I don't know about long-term marriage and relationships, but I know for any relationship to continue, with both parties being relatively content and fulfilled within it, evolution is vital. That doesn't mean always being happy; rather that, as you both naturally change and grow as people, you do so together, whether that is negotiating how you spend time together or apart. I don't often envy marriage, but when I see people in long relationships who work cohesively as a team, and who – crucially – course-correct their lives in accordance to their evolving needs and desires, it seems wonderful.

I found the story of Jada Butler, a physician assistant and therapist, who is married with six children to be one of those. Jada runs a Substack called *The Midlife Nomad*, and I was drawn to her work after reading a post that said, 'Everyone who has ever reimagined her life knows that courage isn't about being fearless but about feeling the trembling in your hands and moving forward anyway.'

She and her husband decided to 'burn their life down' in the United States by selling their possessions and giving the rest to their children. They were looking at places to retire in the US and came across a YouTube video about the healthiest places to live. 'We completed a values worksheet together, recommended by a retirement podcast, and it helped us realise we want to live a life based on our values, rather than conforming to what others expect from us,' Jada said. 'We started digging a bit deeper and then booked a trip to Portugal for a scouting trip. We fell in love.'

Although Jada's husband initially thought she was mad when she first suggested moving, he eventually came round. 'We talked about the pros and cons for hours at a time for months,' she said. 'There was also an element of trusting our instincts. If one person feels passionate about something, the other typically supports that. Once we were in Portugal and both experienced what it was like to be there, everything became clear. He then took the lead, and then I became the one feeling moments of fear.'

Their children were supportive – the youngest graduated at the end of 2025 – and Jada was able to continue her practice online as they travelled. It's the best thing they've done, she said, and her children sometimes come out to visit. 'For me, it was having several friends die unexpectedly young that made me question everything and seriously contemplate my mortality. But we are often defined (and trapped) by our ever-growing collection of stuff that defines our lives. Once we let go and started traveling with just a few items, there was a tremendous sense of freedom and lightness. Now we talk of going to a concert in France or taking our bikes to Spain to ride. Or rent a place in Italy and learn how to cook authentic Italian food. Things and experiences I never would have considered possible now seem within reach.'

When I asked people to tell me how they live outside the status quo, but within the structure of a long-term relationship, photographer Margaret Soraya got in touch. She left Manchester for the Highlands in her twenties, and now, in her early fifties, lives in the Outer Hebrides. Although she has been with her partner Rob for twelve years, they don't live together. 'I met him after my divorce when I still had two young children at home,' she said. 'We always felt that living together would put too much pressure on our relationship. After the divorce, my boys and I had to leave our home, had financial struggles and moved between rented accommodation across Scotland for years. I never wanted my children to go through more upheaval than they had already experienced.'

SHE WANTED MORE

In the beginning, Margaret and Rob lived near each other in Drumnadrochit, but she found herself travelling more and more to Harris for her work, which is a seven-hour drive away. Rob also has a busy job on the mainland. To make the trips affordable, Margaret bought a van to sleep in and would go between the two places. But eventually, after her children left home, she realised she wanted to buy her own small place in Harris.

'Rob struggled with my decision at first, but I knew in my heart that I had to take this chance at my dream and he understood. It was finally my time – to have a home without stress, noise, or pressure. Now, we've found a rhythm that works for us. I often travel back to Drumnadrochit as my life is more flexible than his. We visit each other when we can.'

Life is wonderful, she said. On a good day, her morning begins early with a kayak and her camera, surrounded by seals. 'I wake up on the island, look outside, and see sheep strolling down the road – no cars in sight, just a wild, empty landscape stretching for miles.' Although she struggles with Long Covid and chronic fatigue, it has made her more grateful for what she has.

'My health has led to a beautiful path of self-discovery,' she mused, 'and understanding that space and quiet, protecting my own energy, being creative, not over-caring for others and having a calm life is non-negotiable.'

* * *

My mother isn't a particularly traditional person by South Asian parenting standards, and neither is my father. They have never made my sister or I feel as if we should go down a particular career path or that we should prioritise marriage over our careers.

It was therefore a surprise, around three years ago, when I heard my mother say that it was her wish to see me remarried before she died. We were sitting in her bedroom, the morning sun flooding in and warming my feet. 'I just want to know that someone is taking care of you,' she said, her hair ruffled from sleep, holding a mug of coffee that my father had just given her. I didn't want to get into it, so I settled for a muted scoffing noise. *Pah!* (It was the best I could do under the circumstances.)

I am aware of the contradiction: I am sceptical of marriage and yet I'm the person I am *because* of the long, flowing river of my parents' marriage. They have been together longer than they have been apart. It is remarkable to see them discern true feeling in each other through a mere inflection of tone, or a fleeting glance. Having seen other people's long marriages, I know it is unusual that they still actively love each other, and not in the way one might love an old, worn teddy bear. Of course they argue about the same things they have been disagreeing over for decades, but their love is expressed in a thousand small ways from my dad checking my mother has taken her medication to my mother buying his favourite coffee.

On their fiftieth wedding anniversary in 2024, we were all so caught up with the logistics of organising a big party at home that the import of the occasion didn't hit us until my father held out his hand to my mother in the marquee in their back garden, surrounded by all the people they loved, as her favourite song played (Ed Sheeran's 'Perfect').

Today's lavish weddings contrast starkly with the often-humble ones our parents had. Mine got married in 1974 on a shoestring budget, and there were no such things as sugared almonds, hen dos, three-tier wedding cakes or champagne flutes. This wasn't just an anniversary for my mother; it was a chance for her to have all the things she had seen and dreamed about over the years. And we wanted to give that to her – for all that she had sacrificed and done, all the lives she had blessed with the generosity of her little beating heart, inviting people into her home and so many small acts of kindness. As we watched them dance, my mother's friend wanted to know the song they danced to on their wedding day back in 1974. 'Was it a Bollywood song?' she asked. And with watery eyes, I said: '*This* is their first dance.'

I've borne witness to their love and their marriage, and I also know I will never experience anything like it. I have been lucky to have known a soulmate love, and I have loved other people since Rob. But the two combined is beyond me now. Even if I got married *today*, having a marriage of the same duration as my parents would take me to the age of ninety-five, and the idea of being with another person for that long is unappealing. But it would also be impossible because I am not the person I was before I married Rob, and what I would want from marriage is hard to find in another person – and I don't know if that person exists. It also feels as if I am yearning for something that isn't actually real. The marriages of our parents and grandparents have long been held as the gold standard, an expectation that some of us feel we should strive for, and feel terrible when we don't measure up. But the truth is that for many women in these generations – especially our grandmothers' – leaving wasn't a choice. We romanticise the reality – they didn't necessarily stay because each was living the love story of their lives, but because they had no other way of supporting themselves or their children.

The idea of a man 'taking care of me' is simply that – an idea. It has never, ever been a reality. Even when I was recovering after heart surgery, I needed to go to my mother's house because Rob thought he was doing a good job of taking care of me, and he wasn't. I didn't know it at the time, but his behaviour was erratic because of drug addiction, and I don't have to be understanding or generous about that. He fucked up, he let me down, and he didn't take care of me in the way I needed.

That doesn't mean to say he didn't do a lot in our marriage or that he wasn't caring. He would cook, pick me up from the station, get certain household things done because he was freelance while I was working in an office, sort out things to do with the car, the bins, the heavy lifting. He saw himself in that role and he loved it, as did I. I felt protected – until I didn't. I felt loved until I realised it wasn't enough. In the aftermath I realised that, somewhere along the way, I had made a much bigger compromise than Rob had – and neither of us was aware of it. It was never spoken about, but I knew that running the household and getting things organised was mostly my job. When it came to managing things like his health, it was my job too. I was responsible for making sure we were both okay, which meant that very often no one was taking care of me.

Perhaps that was just my own marriage, but I've listened to many other women talk about their marriages; and at some point, a woman needs to face the fact that, beyond 'in sickness and in health', she will always be giving more, and compromising more, if she wants to get married or stay married.

The veil isn't slipping; it has slipped. When I remember that peace, the thing I long for most, is the thing a man has never been able to give me, it will take a lot for me to ever consider getting married again.

* * *

Writing in *Feminism is for Everybody: Passionate Politics*, the author bell hooks laid out a vision of what marriage could be. It resonated deeply.

'There can be no love when there is domination . . . This vision of relationships where everyone's needs are respected, where everyone has rights, where no one need fear subordination or abuse, runs counter to everything patriarchy upholds about the structure of relationships.

'Marriages built on a sexist foundation are likely to be deeply troubled and rarely last. All recent studies of successful marriages show that gender equity creates a context where each member of the couple is likely to be affirmed. This affirmation creates greater happiness, and, even if the marriage does not last forever, the peer friendship that has been the foundation of the bond continues.'

Although so much is said about marriage being the natural conclusion to finding your ultimate romantic partner, I love the idea of prioritising friendship from the very beginning. It shifts the focus away from the performance of marriage back to the bones of what makes any good relationship – love, respect and mutual values. A common factor in people who co-parent healthily after a breakup is the presence of friendship – whether that is a return to a previously existing friendly bond or building a new one.

Before marriage, asking the right questions to uncover how your partner feels about things is vital. Are you aligned on your ethics? Have you had a chat about your finances? Do you genuinely think your partner would make a good father? Is your partner someone who is open to change? Are they responsible when it comes to their own health?

The reason these questions are important is because the same problems come up over and over again in middle age. Women aren't perfect little angels, but the most common problems in midlife marriages are ones where you feel like your spouse is yet another child you're having to take care of, where they don't take responsibility for their health, where they don't have therapy to deal with the issues that impact you, and where they may not cheat on you but they betray you in small ways such as not supporting you.

That doesn't mean marriage is not worth bothering with. I know men who have taken control of their mental health and pursued therapy. Couples who have tried workshops to improve their sex life after long periods of sexlessness and it has worked. Relationships that have been renegotiated and seen a new lease of life. I also know couples who prioritise spending time alone even though they have children, and that was unheard of in my mother's generation.

I've even met women who want to experiment with their sexuality, for instance, and their husbands have supported them. That actually blew my mind.

I met a woman at an LGBTQ+ event a couple of years ago – let's call her Nadia. She was thirty-five years old and originally from New Delhi. I was intrigued by her journey, as I always am with South Asian queer folk, and she told me that she was bisexual and married. She'd felt this need to explore her sexuality, because she hadn't been able to before she got married. Eventually, she decided to talk to her husband about it. He was understanding and gave her the time she needed. 'I'll take care of the kids,' he said. 'Just go out and have a good time.' The import of it, that a South Asian *man* could be that progressive, gave me immense hope.

And there is hope – lots of it.

But before any of that can happen, you have to believe that you deserve, and are capable of having, a relationship that may not be perfect, but that is gorgeous and complicated and filled with warmth. And that change, the redrawing of lines – even within a marriage – is not just optional, it is vital.

* * *

While there are challenges in any marriage, from child-rearing to finances, one of the biggest problems these days is people feeling stuck. This is partly because we are living longer. For those women who are at least a decade into their marriages and experiencing the same problems over and over again, there tends to be a period in our forties and early fifties where we may think: What the fuck is this? Am I going to have to deal with this until one of us dies, which may very well be a few more decades?

Before it gets to the point of breaking up, it is worth trying a few strategies. Not just because dating apps are a hellhole, but because there may be good things in your partnership that are worth saving.

I talked about this renegotiation process to Katariina Räike, a relationship coach and marriage mentor, based in Finland. One reason I was drawn to her was that she says she can help professional women 'transform' their marriage without their partner ever needing to know. When I think of all the women who feel stuck and silently scream because their male partners refuse to get therapy, I wonder if this might be a good solution. I'm not saying we should let men off doing the work, but something needs to give, in order to overcome the impasse. (I've listened to hours upon hours of conversations with friends who are never going to leave their partners, while their partners are never going to get the help they need.)

'My clients are all women whose partners have already emotionally, sometimes also physically, checked out (they've even left the family home),' Katariina told me. 'Far more often than not, they are able to reconcile, reconnect, and continue on a positive growth path of better communication and deeper closeness than before. So, it absolutely can start with one person. It is not easy, and it does take work, but with the right process and support, it is possible. At the same time, if the commitment is not there, and if it feels easier to stay in resentment and anger, and blame the partner or circumstances, it's not possible.'

The most common problems, she says, are lack of connection, which typically comes from poor communication skills in the marriage, and lack of self-awareness. 'Often it is the simplest things we need and want in our marriage: to feel understood, to feel seen, to know that our partner is on our side and makes us feel safe, and that we know we can trust them no matter what happens.'

In the 'She Wanted More' survey, I asked women who'd been in relationships longer than ten years how they managed to renegotiate their relationships so that they were in a better place. This question prompted some women to realise they had never had this conversation with their partners. Some said they were stuck in relationships where nothing was changing. A significantly higher number of women in their forties and older had divorced because they felt they weren't being listened to.

The women who had completed this renegotiation successfully shared some common solutions. Communication was key, as well as giving each other space. In some cases, that involved living separately, travelling separately or just giving the other person time for their own hobbies. In most cases, they needed to take a long view that this was part of an ongoing process, requiring patience.

'We have been together for eighteen years and have changed infinitely during this time,' wrote Melanie. 'We communicate a lot. When we have pothole months, we take it back to the drawing board. Sometimes this is because I have poor mental health months so it can be a rollercoaster. But our relationship has evolved as part of an ongoing conversation – an honest conversation of trust – and we share similar life choices. I will say, it is hard work. As it should be. And worth it!'

'We have learnt to split bills proportionately,' wrote Sabrina. 'For a long time I tried to keep up – as a feminist I felt I should pay 50/50. But then I realised I would never earn as much and it was okay to ask for things to be fairer. I add value in other ways to the relationship in terms of emotional labour, planning etc.'

Rebecca wrote: 'We've been together twenty-five years and have a foundation of friendship. (We didn't have kids for thirteen years.) There might be less sex now but we understand why, and our relationship is grounded in more than that, although it's still important.'

Negotiating life changes with grace and patience for the other person was also a recurring theme.

'We've both had career changes and have supported each other through those,' wrote Ola. 'We've both experienced parent loss and that makes us kinder and more supportive of each other. Lockdown was a real test and we emerged more empathetic. My husband now works with a young and diverse set of work colleagues and working with younger women has made him more empathetic to the pressures of being a woman. He also knows that ageing as a woman has its own pressures.'

And a reminder that the path isn't always linear.

'Our relationship has opened, closed, opened again, sexually and romantically,' Erin said. 'We have moved cities a few times in search of fulfilling friendships and relationships. We are in constant dialogue.'

'We separated for a while and now are back together,' Immy wrote. 'We have gone back to "date nights" and doing more things together (just us two) such as going to the gym together. Being more honest what pisses us off about each other. Being more honest about finances.'

Kim wrote in with a gentle reminder that this is about love, not who is always right. 'Encouraging each other to follow our dreams (e.g. my husband became a filmmaker in his forties) is what I love the most about our relationship,' she said.

Finally, a beautiful message that gave me hope, from a person with the longest relationship in the survey. 'We have been together forty-two years,' Diana wrote, 'and we always check in with each other. Tell each other if feelings have been hurt, and celebrate the successes. We have each other's back.'

When I read these comments, I feel that love and warmth flowing through. A reminder that marriage isn't perfect, it will not always be enchanting, and that there is no right or wrong way of doing it, as long as you are both happy and feel fulfilled.

It is also a reminder that, while everyone will tell you that marriage is about compromise, it is often framed as having to give up something of yourself. To me, compromise means each person giving a small amount in the pursuit of a common goal, to create harmony, and to allow your lives to move forward. Sometimes it sucks, and you end up giving more than you want. But overall, it should never be about the hollowing out of yourself or endless sacrifice, or the feeling that you are moving further and further away from your centre of gravity. Maybe it did once, when marriage was about survival, but not anymore.

Modern marriage, to me, seems to transcend love. It is wonderful if you have it all, but first and foremost, it seems to be about partnership, respect and alignment of long-term goals. That might sound unsexy, more like a business manifesto than a romantic undertaking. But as I have found, even in the briefest of moments, when you are with the right partner who wants vitality and joy for you more than you even want it for yourself, who says, *I see you, I'm with you, I'll help you, you don't have to do this alone* – when trust exists outside yourself, it offers solace and comfort in a world of rough edges.

CHAPTER FIVE

BREAKUPS, SHAKEUPS AND WTFS

When I was a child, divorce was taboo and rarely spoken about. When it was, the woman bore the brunt of the blame, and I still feel like people do this subconsciously. Whether it was discussing a celebrity's divorce or someone we knew, it slipped in between the words like smoke, as people discussed what had gone wrong. It was never: What did he do? Or not do? It was always about *her*. Even if her husband cheated on her – what was it that *she* did to make him stray? What didn't she do?

I have had heated conversations with friends and family about the reasons why someone's marriage broke down, and was shocked to discover that people would rather blame all sorts of things (even witchcraft) than put the blame on a man. 'Wifely neglect' is also a popular one. 'What else was he supposed to do?' someone asked me, after we'd been discussing a friend who apparently cheated because his wife's job changed and she had to do a lot more business travel. 'Not put his penis into someone else?' I replied drily.

We talk about a woman trying to 'keep' a man, ranging from how she looks to how she behaves – what are the expectations for a man to keep a woman, beyond just existing? Men will say 'money', and perhaps that works with some women, but it is not the basis for most marriages now that women have more financial independence, and it is not enough to sustain a long-term relationship. 'With the rise in female earning, men need to clear a higher bar to be seen as husband material,' Richard V. Reeves writes, in *Of Boys and Men*.

To halt the flurry of paper cuts that people automatically inflict on a woman's identity in divorce, we have to acknowledge two things. Firstly, the unfair power dynamic in heterosexual marriage – that men are allowed to be passive in the relationship, while women must continually find ways to be enchanting. Secondly, we need to understand how that misplaced sense of responsibility, which feeds into the piss-poor expectations we have of men, tends to amplify when we enter into long-term relationships. I once heard someone say that 'a great man in a marriage is at best an average woman' and it made me laugh *and* cry.

I am not pro-divorce or pro-singledom, but I do want women, especially heterosexual women, to know that they are taught to earn worth in the eyes of society by having a man, and therefore have the most to lose if it doesn't work out. If a relationship fails, people will both blame and pity you for it, because a woman alone is a pitiable thing – a shrew, a spinster – while a man alone is a wild stallion living his best Old Spice life. Once, in a supermarket, I was buying myself a bunch of freesias, when the male cashier asked me who they were for. 'Myself,' I exhaled happily. 'Oh that's sad,' he replied. 'A woman having to buy flowers for herself.' All these things combined mean that we end up staying in failing relationships far longer than we should, and we make compromises on things that we really shouldn't – such as who we have children with. I'm not even referring to serious issues such as domestic violence or infidelity; rather the grey area of settling with someone who is just about okay.

I have been this woman, and I have listened to these women. The endless talk about men – what they do, what they don't do, what they haven't done, whether they've messaged, what they mean when they say they want something 'casual but meaningful'. The ongoing fucking dance of how to behave around them in order not to scare them off.

* * *

I have made excuses for men and tried to understand the trauma of what they have gone through, while they have made absolutely no attempt to make room for mine. I have thought about how to make space for them in my life; to move my busy work schedule, knowing they are not doing the same for me. I have had not one, not two but three men in the last four years who have prioritised their work above seeing me, without making any concessions to my many work commitments.

In their friendship groups, men are talking about investments, the holidays they are going on, their plans for world domination, and we are talking about *them*. Looking at their messages under a microscope, searching for a sign they give a fuck about us. I don't want to talk about it anymore. I don't want to be sympathetic about the guy you like who forgot your birthday because he was upset about a work project. The fucking bozo who you caught DMing women online who said he only did it because you weren't giving him enough attention.

Call it peri-menopause, call it decades of hearing the same conversations over and over again, but I'm not listening to it anymore, and neither should you. Stop allowing other people to pressure you into making it work with someone who should be writing a daily gratitude list that you're in their life, rather than scooting around commitment like a dog with worms. Stop accepting behaviour you would NEVER accept if your friend was going through it. Enough! Reclaim your time, your sanity and your energy.

A common pushback from women stuck in these shitty relationships is 'I don't want to be alone'. And I want to say to them, 'But it sounds like you already *are* alone.' I have certainly experienced it. Even someone as beloved as Rob was to me made me feel like a stranger in my own life when I considered what I was reduced to: willing to accept scraps. At one point, things had got so bad, all I wanted was to be able to go for coffee with my husband in the daytime. When it finally happened, when he was in recovery, I wanted to cry. It was such a small thing, that most people wouldn't think twice about, and yet it was enormous. I'd just never thought that either of us would be reduced to being grateful for a mere coffee together, when our friends were off on long romantic weekends in the countryside.

SHE WANTED MORE

While there were significant factors behind Rob's behaviour that were not his fault, the thing that broke our marriage was the constant lying and his inability to accept that he couldn't fix it all by himself. It just took me a long time to realise I had reached the point of no return, because women have been taught that betrayal has a specific shape – cheating, abuse – and so they don't recognise the many other betrayals that take place.

I don't want women to leave their partners unnecessarily. What I want is for them to be able to leave without having to be broken to realise it. For them to know that if they are miserable, leaving is a possibility, and that many women go on to have better, more fulfilled lives rather than the hollow, empty shell they fear it will become. Yes, 27% of women regret divorce, but 73% do not, and that is despite a woman's income falling by about 40% after divorce.[17] You do not have to spend years in misery trying to gather enough reasons to leave so that society won't judge you. Fuck society. Society will judge you for everything, from eating croissants to how you hold your fork, to getting married to having a child, to having more children, to not raising your children correctly.

When I asked people who were unhappy in their marriages why they continued to stay with their partners, judgement from society was a factor, as was worrying about money. One person said: 'Can't face dating again. And I'm too old to find someone else to try for a baby with.' But ending a relationship might lead to something better.

In the 'She Wanted More' survey, Erica wrote: 'I got married in my mid-twenties and my life was on a very safely mapped-out path. My divorce at the age of twenty-nine – my husband had an affair – was the darkest and most painful thing I've been through, but it taught me so much and made me a better, wiser, more compassionate person to myself and others. It also opened my life up to being so much bigger and more adventurous than it might have been if I'd stayed married and had kids in my early thirties as I had planned.

'Many of the best experiences of my life are because I went through that relationship breakdown and had to open myself up to a different path. I've had another long-term relationship since then which ended last year so I haven't got the loving partner and kids I thought I would have, but I do have a very rich and wonderful life and a lot of inner strength, independence and wisdom that I gained from my divorce.'

Trying to make a relationship work with someone you don't love may be possible if you come from a culture that has arranged marriage within it, and you know what you are getting into. But if you subscribe to the soulmate ideology, you don't realise the scale of that sacrifice until you are older and dealing with a number of issues relating to your partner, and parenting with them. I have seen men consume the dreams of women this way over and over again, and I have seen women punish men for not being the person they never were anyway.

* * *

Before we continue, it's important to give context by mentioning that in this chapter we'll mainly be discussing heterosexual marriage and the dynamics that exist within it.

SHE WANTED MORE

This is partly because in countries such as the UK and US, gay marriage was only legalised in 2013 and 2015 respectively, and the problems that have arisen in heterosexual marriage – based on centuries of restrictive gender norms – don't have exact parallels in homosexual relationships.

There is also a lack of understanding around the flexibility of how relationships can be arranged that is absent in many heterosexual couples. Referencing the jealousy and protectiveness that Harari writes about in *Sapiens* in relationships between women and men, and how that has developed/intensified over time, most heteros in my social circle cannot conceive of open relationships, while they are much more prevalent among my gay friends. While of course there are open heterosexual relationships, they are in the minority and are not generally considered acceptable in mainstream society.

The reason why it is important to have a long think about marriage, and whether or not you want to be legally tied to someone, as laid out in the previous chapter, is that divorce is hard, complicated and expensive. The median length of a marriage between people of the opposite sex, says the Office of National Statistics, is now 12.7 years.[18]

I understand that's not what you're thinking about when you're in love (having been there and done that). But litmus-testing these parts of your relationship is important because it will get harder if you don't know how you both feel about certain topics such as financial dependence, having children, and your careers. Sometimes these things sit in conflict. For instance, if you have a high-powered job, do you want a partner who has a similar job or do you want someone who is going to have more mental and physical space for you? I see some women struggling with this a lot – where they want someone who has power and money but also want someone who spends a lot of time with them – and the two are not always compatible.

Women tend to initiate divorce more than men, and in the US it applies to 70% of divorces, while in the UK it is around 62%.[19] No-fault divorces, which were introduced in the UK in 2022, were a step change for women because previously there needed to be evidence of wrongdoing, whether that was abuse or infidelity. (Which also underpinned the guilt a woman might feel if she wanted to leave the marriage for other reasons, as they were seen as less valid.) 'No-fault' means that marriages can end more amicably, and in the UK around 42% of marriages end in divorce.[20]

Does that mean women are trigger-happy around divorce? Of course not. It is a huge undertaking, and one that most likely involves years of consideration and cost.

But perhaps the biggest factor to be considered *before* you get married is that, while women do better in terms of mental wellbeing after divorce, in the long term they can end up worse-off financially. This is not just because of the gender pay gap, which means that covering the bills solo, including childcare, is more difficult, but also because of the financial literacy gap – which includes things like women being more risk-averse around investments. Mothers who take time off during their marriage to do more of the childcare may also find this impacts their ability to return to work at a later stage;

and without the financial structure of a marriage, they may have a harder time of it.

In an article for *The Guardian* written by Tracy McVeigh, Nigel Shepherd, chair of mediation organisation Resolution, said: 'There's this perception that men feel they get taken to the cleaners. Like any generic perception, it's trite. Women do worse out of divorce, but I don't think it's the particular failing of the system that penalises women; it's more that the ability to recover financially after divorce reflects the wider inequality in society. A couple who have been married 30 years and divorce in their mid-fifties, may split everything equally, but there is still a built-in inequality in the ability to rebuild from that point. You go into it unequal and end up unequal.'[21]

Does that mean you shouldn't get divorced or leave your partner? Not at all. It merely means that before and during marriage, no matter how happy and certain you are, you should be sure to maintain a baseline level of independence around your finances. And that whatever you are striving for, whether it is making your relationship work, or making the tough decision to leave it, you're remembering to take care of yourself financially within the emotional storm of it all.

World-renowned relationship therapist Esther Perel says staying or going is one of the most common questions she receives as a therapist. 'Relational Ambivalence – those contradictory thoughts and feelings of love and hate, attraction and disgust, excitement and fear – makes us constantly wonder: should I stay or should I go?' she writes in her blog *Letters from Esther*. 'The resulting whiplash is exhausting, not only for the people in the relationship but the people around it.' It is a complicated topic, she says, and one that doesn't always have a straight answer. But the way to snap out of it is to take a stance, and see what reaction comes up.

Esther uses the example of when she was in her own relationship ambivalence with an ex-boyfriend, and a couples therapist suggested they should break up. Although they did end up splitting, Esther called the therapist to complain that she shouldn't have said anything. 'I'll never forget what she told me. Her position was that, when you work with couples frozen in ambivalence, taking a stance for them can break the cycle. If they agree (with your advice to break up), they'll experience relief in the permission they couldn't give themselves. If they disagree, they'll align against you instead of each other.'

I think a similar effect could be produced by asking yourself what your friends and family think of you as a couple. If they knew the full scope of your relationship, would they want you to be with your partner? And if the answer is no, perhaps it's worth seeing if agreement or indignation comes up as your reaction.

A phrase I hear often from women who continue in unhappy relationships is: 'I can't bear to date again.' And to that I want to say – *if you can bear to feel unsupported by him, to have him spend money on stupid shit when it should be spent on your home or kids, be called a nag when you're just trying to get him to do 50% of the life admin, have to coddle him around his health, have your peace disrupted on a weekly if not daily basis, then you can bear to be single.*

There are so many women in these types of relationships

that there is even a phrase for it: 'married but single'. A couple of years ago, it was posted as a hashtag on Twitter/X and hundreds of people posted comments about how they might as well be doing it alone, from childcare to celebrating their own wins, saying their partner is someone they take care of, rather than someone who does their share.

'One of the things I couldn't bear,' wrote Deena in the survey, 'was doing everything alone (having the load fall on me), and yet not actually being alone. I also found it very difficult sharing a small space with another adult. It's not that I don't value compromise, but we are so often bending and contorting ourselves for the benefit of the men in our lives and I have no interest in doing that ever again. I enjoy being able to do what I want (within reason, as I am a single mum), and live as myself, just me.'

* * *

In South Asian culture, which tends to be more conservative about marriage than white British or American culture, divorce is less common. South Asia has some of the lowest divorce rates in the world – in India it is just 1%. Immigrant South Asians in America have some of the highest marriage rates and the lowest divorce rates.

However, in the UK, divorce among South Asians is increasing – according to the *Asian Voice* newspaper which cited recent figures. 'Approximately 10% of British Pakistani Muslims and Indian Sikhs are now separated or divorced. Around 8% of Bangladeshi Muslims, 7% of Indian Muslims, and 6% of Indian Hindus have also experienced marital separation,' they said.[22] This is in comparison to 20% of white Brits and 27% of black British Caribbean people.

I can just imagine some elderly Asian uncle bemoaning the 'westernisation' of South Asians as the reason for this increase, but the fact is that we are simply catching up with the wider change in gender roles. While preserving one's culture is important, I have no interest in holding on to beliefs and practices that disproportionately make a woman's life worse. Sandi Silva, a counsellor from Melbourne who specialises in providing therapy for South Asian women in Australia, spoke to ABC about the worry over cultural backlash.

'These women have over-stayed in loveless marriages, and in more severe cases, marriages where they were victim to abuse and mistreatment,' she said. 'Divorced women . . . are labelled as selfish, unwilling to compromise or unable to tolerate the challenges that come with marriage – regardless of the circumstances around the divorce. This messaging implies that if you can't meet these cultural expectations, there must be something wrong with you. It suggests that you are the problem rather than the narrow cultural expectations.'[23]

While as an adult I've met a number of (mostly white) people whose parents divorced when they were younger – when I was younger, I only knew one divorced person, and that was my mother's oldest sister Meera.

I was born in England, but when I was six, my family decided to relocate back to Bangalore, India. My father stayed in England while trying to sell the house my parents owned, and my mother, sister and I built a life in a tiny but beloved flat tucked away on a leafy avenue behind a busy main street.

SHE WANTED MORE

Over the course of five years, I got to grow up alongside my cousins, and be absorbed into the warm, flowing matrix of an extended family.

During that time, my aunt Meera lived in the much bigger, noisier metropolis of New Delhi, and we would see her from time to time. I didn't know much about her, other than that she was easy-going and I liked her; but I also knew she was divorced, and that her children lived with their father. In retrospect, this was an unusual arrangement – more often than not, children tend to live with their mothers after a divorce. But she had such a gorgeous relationship with her children, who adored her, that it didn't seem strange.

In the way that certain ideas arrive by osmosis, I knew as a child that divorce was 'a bad thing'. It meant something had gone terribly wrong if a woman chose to be divorced, rather than be with her husband. Which seemed weird because Meera Auntie didn't seem broken to me, or a figure of pity. She seemed especially beloved by her friends, and she was so much fun.

Over the years, we didn't see each other much. We moved back to England, and then she moved to work in an ashram in Kerala. In recent years, however, that has changed. Some years ago, she moved back to Bangalore and now she, my mother and their youngest sister Indu all live within two streets of each other. Although my parents only live there seasonally during England's winter months, I've made several trips to Bangalore in the past ten years which has enabled me to see more of her, as well as her home.

One thing strikes me as significant – compared to every

one of her peers who are married and live with their spouses, Meera Auntie is the least anxious, and the most peaceful. You feel it in her home from the moment you arrive. She is not involved in other people's business. She leaves social events when she wants, and she pursues the things that give her pleasure, from playing cards to spending time with her children. It gives me something to aspire to, a roadmap of what my life might look like when I am her age. It's not that I don't admire my own mother or other women of her generation, but my life looks nothing like theirs. And yet, wasn't this the thing that everyone spoke about in hushed tones? A divorced woman without a man – how could she ever be happy and content? And yet, she is. Whether or not she knows it, she has been so important in helping me to see a positive future for myself.

When I thought about writing this book, I realised how little I knew about her earlier life, and how much of it was cobbled together from scraps of memory. I knew she was divorced and that her ex-husband had remarried, but I didn't know why. On an impromptu trip to Bangalore in early 2025, I went to her flat for tea and a chat, and what she told me left me stunned. Especially because, from what little I remembered, I'd had the impression that it was somehow her fault that things hadn't worked out.

Her husband, she said, was making a lot of money and they were living in a five-bedroomed bungalow with their children. As time went on, my youngest uncle Shyam was due to get married, and Meera Auntie and her husband were meant to attend the wedding together. But they had a huge fight, and she ended up going alone. By the time she got back, her husband asked for a divorce. He'd been having an affair.

He'd had affairs before, but after a lot of discussion, my aunt realised she didn't want to force him to be in a marriage he clearly didn't want to be in. 'I thought, there's no point in holding a gun to his back and making him stay if he doesn't want to. But people back in Bangalore blamed me and said: *Why did you give him a divorce?*'

While she was still in shock at the dissolution of her marriage, her ex-husband managed to convince her to sign away her right to alimony and give custody of the children to him, promising that she'd always have access and that he'd give her money. This turned out to be conditional. He could cut it off any time he liked, and he sometimes did. At one point, he threatened to kick her out of the house he was paying rent for if she didn't do what he asked, so she packed her bags, gave him the keys and walked out.

'He told his brother: I'm going to break her pride. That I was too arrogant. He expected Indian women to be subservient. And I told myself that's something that's not going to happen. He's not going to break me, no matter what.' Even though it was decades later, I saw the fierce defiance still shining in my aunt's eyes, which was all the more remarkable because of the time this was happening in.

Her story started to spread through the community, and it ended up being reduced to: *her husband asked for a divorce, and she gave it to him.* 'It gave the impression that I was unbothered,' she said, 'which was not true. We were together for seven years and I thought we were a happy family. Yes, you have fights, but who doesn't? And when I was asked about why I gave him a divorce, I said – what was I supposed to do? What kind of marriage would that have been?'

She was determined not to feel ashamed about it and went back to attending social events. 'I thought, I'm not going to hide away. I haven't done anything wrong.' At first, she said she got some looks from people, but then it died down, and her life grew up around her. She worked hard, visited her children, and she always managed to make it work even without a stable income. Reading the *Bhagavad Gita*, the ancient Hindu text, gave her immense comfort in figuring out the big life lessons. Many years later, she started working for the Chinmaya Mission, which we called the 'ashram', but it was actually a research centre specialising in Sanskrit studies. They also hosted various camps and needed someone to take care of things. That person was my aunt, and for twelve years, she lived in a little green paradise surrounded by learning.

When I told Meera Auntie about how my sister and I perceived her, that she is someone who has paved her own way and also seems to be at peace, she looked surprised. 'I do have this positive way of looking at things, that things will just take care of themselves. Yes, there'll be ups and downs, but I'm not going to worry about it, because worry is not going to solve the problem. This is the happiest time of my life. I don't have any responsibilities. My children are grown and take care of me financially, and I don't have to worry about anything. I'm just leading a happy, carefree life now.'

* * *

SHE WANTED MORE

When I was a young adult, divorce was something that happened to other people – especially American or British white people. Even when it started filtering through to a couple of cousins in my late twenties, I never imagined it was something that would happen to myself or my sister Priya, until it did.

In 2009, Rob and I had been dating for nearly a year, and I'd stayed at his house in Streatham overnight. I'd forgotten my phone in the flat I shared with my best friend Mal fifteen minutes down the road. I came home in the morning to see ten missed calls from my sister – her husband had asked her for a divorce. I was in shock. This must be a mistake. I'd just come back from visiting them after they'd moved to New York from London. We'd gone to the West Village and bought cupcakes, explored little speakeasies. I spent a lot of time at their home over the years, and my brother-in-law was like an actual brother. Until he wasn't, and I learned how divorce could instantly make strangers of the people we'd once loved as family.

Although my sister and I are close to the point of symbiosis, we didn't talk much about her divorce back then. Time sanded down the prickly parts, and she met her second husband Shihab (who was a friend of mine) and filled her world with new life in the form of Leela. While I staple my pain to my outsides, she holds it in tightly like a clam, and there were things I wanted to know about.

When I asked about her decision to get married in her late twenties, she said that our mother and the women of her generation seemed to have so much clarity and purpose that stemmed from their status as mothers and married women. When I interviewed my mother Jayalaxmi about the decisions that had shaped her life as a young woman, she said that in some ways life was easier for her generation of women. They they had fewer choices and didn't have the luxury of agonising over their identity, so in some ways they were clearer about who they were.

'I thought I would never reach that level of certainty about how I was going to live my life, and maybe that uncertainty meant that I married too early,' Priya said. 'That sense of "I guess I should be doing this then". I felt as if marriage was a route into a life of being a grown-up, and then you'd buy a house and all of the other trappings that come with being in a marriage, especially a heterosexual marriage. It felt like it would cement me as an adult in some way, which now seems ludicrous, thinking about it.'

A few months after Priya got divorced, I got engaged to Rob. We were at such different life stages, which may also explain why we didn't talk much about what was going on, but one thing was very clear: she was a different person after the divorce. When we were growing up, Priya was always known as the one who was soft-natured – a sweetheart who would do whatever she was asked. After the divorce, she found her voice, and it was strong, purposeful and loud. And adventurous.

She ended up trying so many new things that would previously have scared her senseless. My favourite was when she started taking driving lessons in her late thirties, having failed her test in her teens. She not only passed but hired an eleven-seater people carrier on a family holiday, drove

SHE WANTED MORE

it all the way from France to Italy AND parallel-parked the fucker.

'Although I got divorced nearly fifteen years ago,' Priya said, 'so many women still feel constrained by the same societal norms I did. "Well, this is the hand I either chose or was dealt and I'm just going to live it." And then when I got divorced, it was literally like – imagine a sedated dragon and the sedative wore off. And then she sleepily wakes up and realises, oh, I can actually break these shackles.'

After her divorce, a big part of her awakening was leaving London and temporarily moving to India. 'As mad as that year was,' she said, 'it was a necessary metamorphosis and a "phoenix rising" moment, where if I'd stayed in London and just kept everything the same or made my life very comfortable, I know that change wouldn't have happened.'

At the time, it didn't feel like an empowering rush. In fact, it felt like death. 'It sounds dramatic, but it almost felt like I'd died and become a ghost. I was breathing, so life was clearly continuing, but it seemed unfathomable that it was.'

The honesty her divorce delivered around how she lived her life deeply impacts her today for the better, including her current relationship.

'I knew that I could never again be in a life that didn't serve me,' she said. 'And it's not to say that everything that's happened is exactly how I wanted it. There's always compromise, especially if you're married or in a relationship. And definitely when you're a mum.

'I've just dealt with so many years of being not just a woman, but a brown woman, having people undermine me, underestimate me, not take my thoughts and feelings into account, or my opinions, and I got to a point where I said: no more. I'm not willing to make myself small, to be palatable anymore. The older I've gotten, the more I'm willing to say that compassion for myself has to come first.'

* * *

Recalling the conversations with my aunt and sister fills me with hope, and gladness for them for finding their joy. When it comes to my aunt Meera, tracing the line from when her entire world imploded in her thirties to the present day in her mid-seventies, it is clear how full a life can become, even when it feels like everything is over.

I was especially interested in what she had to say about the impact on her children. She said that around the time of the divorce, people asked her to consider staying with her husband because of the effect a split would have on the kids (which must have been galling, given that she hadn't asked for the divorce). But she knew unequivocally that she could not force someone to be in a marriage, and that it would not benefit her children either – which was an insight far ahead of its time. I'm not sure of the impact it has had on them; I can only comment on what I have witnessed, and – apart from being two of the most fun-loving cousins in my family – the love they have for their mother is vast.

Children are an undeniably important factor in divorce. From the survey and anecdotally, some women said they wouldn't be in their marriages if it wasn't for their children. Some of that may be for financial reasons, and because the burden of raising children as a single parent feels too heavy. But, interestingly, one of the recurring answers to the question of 'what women wished for their mothers' was for them to have exited marriages that clearly weren't working for them, but which they persisted in for the sake of the children. 'I wish she'd chosen herself and built some identity outside of being a mother and wife,' Greta wrote about her mother in the survey.

While it may seem like a necessary sacrifice to create a stable home for your children, giving up on your own happiness doesn't guarantee you'll save your marriage. 'We are now divorcing after forty-one years of marriage,' wrote Cara in the survey. 'My husband walked out two years ago and left me for a close friend of mine. He has lost his home, our joint business, his three adult children and the three grandchildren who have been born since he departed. I wish he could have communicated what his unhappiness looked like.'

Although there are studies showing that children of divorced parents are more likely to be emotionally unstable, engage in sexually risky behaviour and end up in poverty, according to a 2019 article in the *World Psychiatry* journal, most are shown to be more resilient and have no obvious psychological problems compared to people with married parents.[24] And when considering the negative effects, these are not just due to marital instability, but are down to a number of factors, from ethnicity to income. The US-based study found, for instance, that Hispanic and black children of divorce are less emotionally impacted than white children because extended family and community step in to help raise them.

Besides, children who grow up surrounded by an unhappy marriage are not unmarked by the experience. Writing in *Psychology Today*, Sylvia L. Mikucki-Enyart explained how it creates three problems – alliances (where a child sides with one parent), parentification (where one parent subconsciously relies on their child for their emotional needs), and replicating the poor modelling they have seen in their parents' relationships, in their own.[25]

'I left after seventeen years of marriage,' wrote Temi in the survey, 'as I felt unseen and unappreciated and was sick of supporting someone else's achievements. My divorce has been very hard as we are all good people. But I genuinely feel I've mirrored many strong things for my fifteen-year-old daughter.'

One of the most uplifting stories I came across recently was that of Suja Vairavanathan, forty-two, who divorced her husband after twenty years of marriage, and then entered into a relationship with another woman, who was also her best friend. She has two sons aged twenty and sixteen, and both of them still live with her ex-husband, but they are supportive of her choices. Her story was unusual because, while there are a lot of 'coming out while older' stories on TikTok, they are rarely South Asian women, let alone Tamil women – who I feel a close affinity to because our cultures are a lot more similar than other parts of the subcontinent.

Suja didn't leave her marriage because she realised she was gay, she told me. Her marriage had issues of its own. 'All I know is that I came out of a marriage that had been over for a long time,' she said, 'and realised that actually my best friend had all the qualities that I wanted in a partner, and that I was in love with her. I have never looked at her and thought, "I can't love her because she's a woman". She has always known she is queer. I just love who she is and who she makes me be.'

They've been together for two years now, but it hasn't been easy. Suja is estranged from most of her family, and some friends have had problematic responses, with one saying maybe the trauma of her marriage 'made her gay'. Such reactions are depressingly unsurprising, but Suja sees her coming out as a blessing in disguise and has made a lot of new friends, in addition to keeping some of her older friends who have been supportive.

Although her oldest son finds it hard that she's with someone who isn't his dad regardless of gender, her youngest son has been a beacon of hope in supporting her. 'We found ourselves at Berlin Pride,' she said, 'when my son and I happened to be in Berlin for a post-GCSE trip, and he was so interested in what was going on.'

When I asked her if she had advice for other women around finding the courage to live the life they want, she said: 'It's never ever too late. I spent twenty years in a marriage that I knew was not working. I stayed for the children. For my parents. For my siblings. For society. And when I left, apart from my children, no one else was there. And guess what? I didn't die. I didn't vanish into thin air. In fact, I started two businesses. Built up a community, a safe space. And I am the happiest I've ever been.'

I wouldn't have resonated with Suja's story ten, even twenty years ago, but I do now. I am drawn to it because it reminds me that life doesn't work out the way you think it will – it can actually be something better. I love my aunt's ideology because all we can do is make the right choices for now. Maybe you'll regret leaving your partner, maybe you won't. Maybe the door doesn't ever fully close, and maybe it does. All I know is that I have listened and held enough people's stories to realise that change is inevitable, and that's not always a bad thing.

'I'm divorced,' wrote Shay in the survey, 'but back with my husband after seven years separated. I learnt a lot living independently and realised how much I could do alone (without a man), and how confident and strong I am in my own company. I will never be worried now for the future to live alone if needed. My life is great having my ex-husband back in it as my partner, but I have also found many positives being single and living just with my son.'

We are always searching for absolutes in matters of the heart, which is an organ in flux, but perhaps the horizon we should be steering for is peacefulness, whether that is with someone or alone.

CHAPTER SIX

THE RENEGOTIATION OF MOTHER AND MOTHERHOOD

It feels slightly strange to be discussing motherhood as an identity, given that I am not one myself; so in this chapter I will take a back seat and hand over to people who know a lot more about it than I do. Although I have tried to compensate for my blind spots, I may have missed some, and I would recommend following and reading the work of people who work actively to discuss their identity as mothers, from author and podcaster Candice Brathwaite (who writes and talks about black motherhood) to actress Giovanna Fletcher to podcaster and former magazine editor Lorraine Candy (who talks about teenagers and midlife).

I also wanted to include accounts of diverse motherhood, not just people with male partners, and we'll dig into some of the ways they interpret parenting.

Many of the people who took my survey expressed such

delight and pride in their children, particularly when they demonstrated things like kindness. They also highlighted 'completing the circle' – so it wasn't just the recognition of what they gave their children, but also what their children gave them. The fact that Gen Alpha and Z are already so much more aware and advanced around things like racism, homophobia and mental health has had a trickle effect upwards, helping parents to question their own beliefs and feel empowered around their mental wellbeing. The other day, a fifty-something woman told me she was taking a duvet day, and I know that wasn't a phrase she was taught when she was younger.

However, the shorthand version of what motherhood traditionally denotes – all-consuming sacrifice – has been the subject of many contemporary conversations around identity in order to create more oxygen and freedom for women. Not just in terms of redressing the huge amount of labour and service a mother is 'supposed' to offer, but in terms of mothers proactively seeking joy and allowing themselves to enjoy it, in a way our mothers didn't feel able to do. 'They bring me deep joy and exasperation at the same time,' wrote Sophie, about her children, in the survey. 'I wouldn't be without them, yet I feel my freedom is compromised. The duality of being a mother can sometimes be overwhelming.'

The impression I am left with is that it's not about reclaiming yourself 'despite' being a mother, but about being able to hold all the parts of yourself together in a way that doesn't deny or subsume who you are.

'Having kids was a weird combo of stress and boredom ... and a sort of pure love, plus fear, plus hope,' wrote Claire in the survey. 'A friend of mine, many years ago, said, "I will not be defined by my children!" I think I am a bit defined by them, in spite of myself, and sort of don't mind? But also want to find more of my own definition here in my third act.'

It is a prickly subject. Some women who feel very strongly defined by motherhood may see suggestions for them to get other interests as an attack, or that wanting to spend all their time and energy on their children is now viewed as a bad thing. It seems to me that there are ebbs and flows in all of this. It makes sense that you might want to devote yourself entirely to your children when they are small, but seems precarious to continue with the same intensity of devotion as they get older. Not least because pinning your identity to just one thing places too much weight on your children to generate your sense of fulfilment and happiness, but also because it doesn't allow you to adapt as life changes. If everything hinges on them, what happens when they leave home, or if your relationship breaks up, or if they leave the country?

Candice Brathwaite, who was a stay-at-home mum during her early pregnancies, said: 'Early on . . . I reminded my husband that this is only for a time – by "this" I meant playing a more traditional role of being a SAHM who kept things ticking on the home front.

'Most women get "stuck" in a role that provides a service to everyone but themselves. Suddenly, the kids are flying the nest, and they have nothing for themselves, be that a hobby or a career that they are proud of. That really scared me, so I was very vocal about my willingness to pause my dreams but never defer them.'

On the podcast of one of my favourite sexual health, dating and relationship influencers *Lalala Let Me Explain* (their identity is anonymous), the stand-up comedian Laura Smyth, who also has a Radio 4 show *Your Mum*, talked about the importance of taking time for yourself, and friendship. 'More than any (other) factor of how a young woman, or anyone, knows how to treat themselves is how a mother treats herself,' she said. 'Not how a mother treats them. My mum would never have done stuff for herself, and you didn't know you could go out and take your place in the world. For me, it was "you work and you're a mum". It took me being ill to go "I could go on holiday or go to a spa. I can go to things that are not about mothering or working but are just for me." And I want my daughters to know that's what they can do. And that your friends matter.'

As someone without children, it has been important for me to proactively understand what it is like for friends and family who are mothers. Mainly because when I didn't ask questions and just made assumptions, I often got quite a one-dimensional impression of motherhood. It wasn't easy to do this when their children were very small, and their time and energy were non-existent, but as they started to emerge from the fog, those conversations have also been a vital part of understanding how my presence in their life matters. I might not have parenting tips, but I can see how I play a part in helping them to have fun and talk about things other than their children. I've seen over time how this has been a vital part of how they reconnect with themselves.

The friendships that have endured are the ones where they

SHE WANTED MORE

want to hold on to something that is beyond their children. The ones that haven't are ones where their worlds are very small, where they are unable to prioritise themselves. It feels awful to give up on someone, but – given that the oxygen of friendship is reciprocity – both people in a friendship have needs and it cannot all be one-way.

The former Chief Marketing Officer for Netflix and Chief Brand Officer for Uber, Bozoma Saint John, has spoken a lot about this. Bozoma is American-Ghanaian and has a teenage daughter, Lael. She lost her youngest daughter Eve prematurely, and her husband Peter died of cancer in 2013. 'I'm the most important person to me,' she said, talking to Luvvie Ajayi Jones on the podcast *Can't Wait to Hear from You*, 'and I actually counsel my daughter on that too. We don't play that thing of "who is the most important person?" I'm the most important person to me, and she's the most important person to herself. In doing so, I hope what I am teaching her, and what she's seeing in me, is that I'm prioritising my own happiness, my own joy, my own fulfilment, my own satisfaction so that I am a better mother to her. I'm a better friend to you. I'm a better daughter to my parents.'

The person closest to me who has shown me the importance of prioritising your own needs within motherhood, and the complexities around identity, is my sister Priya, who wrote a book called *Motherland: What I've Learnt about Parenthood, Race and Identity*.

'Very early on,' she said, 'I remember a friend saying to me, oh, maternal guilt never leaves you. And I remember feeling quite determined that I would try hard not to feel guilty and to examine the guilt when it came up.

'I fought against the idea that mothers have to completely give their lives over to their kids, because I don't think you can. Like, you can't have the Earth orbiting the sun if the sun is just going to give everything up, because then the Earth doesn't exist in relation to it. So in order for Leela to be okay and to be happy and for me to have the capacity to look after her, I do have to put myself first and make sure I'm okay. And sometimes that kind of delineation is a bit porous, where I am giving more for her because if there's a choice between her being okay or me being okay, then I will lean towards her being okay, but not at the complete cost of myself.'

I've seen how hard Priya works to make space for herself, as well as making sure she is there for Leela. She's attempted solo holidays, gone on trips with friends, and carved out time in the mornings for the gym. After I wrote *Stronger*, I started to get messages from mothers who were taking up strength training and were letting me know how empowering they'd found it. My friend Shabana, who has a teenage daughter, is someone who does an immense amount for other people but fiercely protects her weekends for weightlifting sessions in the gym. 'Saturday mornings used to be all about catching up on life admin and juggling mum duties,' she said, 'but now my lifting club is a non-negotiable priority. It's a guilt-free hour that I make time for each week because the benefits (feeling stronger mentally and physically) far outweigh any short-term scheduling challenges. It's the sense of community that keeps me hooked.'

SHE WANTED MORE

When I asked mothers on Instagram how they made time for themselves and what they enjoyed doing, physical activity was the most common answer – going to the gym, long walks, swimming, Pilates, yoga, playing golf, calisthenics. Reading alone was another one, and relatively low cost. One single mother said that while taking the time is a luxury considering she is raising two children and working full-time, reading relaxes her.

'One of the greatest disservices that we do for women,' Priya said, 'is to subconsciously and consciously tell women that being a good mother means you always have to put your kid first, and that isn't true. Your kid is always important to you, even when they are being an absolute nightmare, but they cannot always be first, or even most of the time, because then you're not going to be okay and then you're not really going to be able to look after them. And I can genuinely say that while I may have regret around certain things, I don't have guilt around that.'

* * *

For some people who are struggling with their identities as mothers, it may be helpful to distinguish between actual mothering and the institution of motherhood.

Poet and essayist Adrienne Rich wrote, in *Of Woman Born: Motherhood as Experience and Institution*, that she aimed to 'distinguish between two meanings of motherhood, one superimposed on the other: the potential relationship of any woman to her powers of reproduction and to children; and the institution, which aims at ensuring that that potential –

and all women – shall remain under male control.' We only have to look at recent events in the United States concerning reproductive rights, specifically abortion rights, as an example of the latter.

Two things offer hope in a world where women are pressured around how they have children, and raise them. The first is how differently I see today's fathers parent their children, both in terms of having conversations about fatherhood and the amount of time they spend with them. Consider that we now have influencer dads and podcasters talking about fatherhood with each other, compared to my father's time, when they didn't discuss it at all.

The second is the seismic change created by mothers my age, and in their fifties, trying to break certain toxic cycles around gender roles for girls and how they themselves are navigating motherhood as an identity.

Part of that – to reference Rich's words about the mythology of motherhood – is because while women may love their children dearly, they are starting to wake up to the fact that they are not bad mothers if they also do things for themselves. While they may not be the same person they were before motherhood, they are still a person with their own wants and needs that are not centred around their children.

Although there has been a shift in the way gender roles are assigned, there are still some big, pervasive issues to contend with. According to a 2023 data dive by Ipsos, 41% of 48,000 people surveyed across fifty different markets still think a woman's main role is to be a good mother and wife.[26] Again – it doesn't mean that marriage and motherhood can't be part of a person's life goals, but for a woman's purpose to be so inextricably tied to men and her reproductive ability feels so regressive, and leaves women who haven't chosen either in social purgatory.

Seeing women visibly reclaim themselves has been an essential part of expanding what motherhood can be, and this impacts all women – not just those with children. Of course, a lot depends on the robustness of a person's support system, and money is always a factor, but one of the areas I have seen change in is travel. Mothers generally didn't travel on their own when I was growing up. But it's different now – whether it's my own sister, or influencers such as Katherine Ormerod, who have spoken about solo travel without their children, or women who've told me about the day trips or afternoons they gift themselves without their kids being around.

When I wrote about solo day trips, a woman messaged me to say that, every year, she leaves her kids at home and stays in a hotel room for a night, ordering room service and reading her book in peace. Listening to these stories felt important to understand how women were renegotiating motherhood for themselves, and why. 'Part of it,' my sister told me, 'is because as girls and as women, we are taught to shelve our needs behind what someone else needs or is asking for.'

* * *

When we are examining the concept of 'She Wanted More' and applying it to motherhood, it feels important to break down what that means. Motherhood is not a monolith – it can take many different forms beyond biologically creating a child. And mothers may have a vast spectrum of incomes, lifestyles and identities, all of which carry their own benefits and challenges. For instance, motherhood for black women and all that it entails, from healthcare to raising black children in a world that adultifies them, will carry significant differences to motherhood for a white British woman.

When we are considering factors such as income, according to a 2022 study by *The Guardian* and the Institute for Fiscal Studies, half of all single parents in the UK are living in poverty, and 90% of these households are run by women.[27] They collectively have 3.1 million children, which accounts for one-fifth of the child population in the country.

It's not as simple as saying 'have a bubble bath and take time for yourself'. Some mothers don't have a village to help out, and they don't have the money to go on holiday with their kids – let alone take one for themselves. 'Parenting is hard, particularly when you are the only one doing it, unsupported,' wrote Laura in the survey. 'I have so much self-doubt and I feel the pressure of raising a human.'

Wanting more for yourself as a mother may simply mean reconnecting in small ways with the parts of you that aren't for someone else. That reminds you that you're a separate person who exists. 'My child has taught me to be kind to myself in a way that I never have been before,' she added. 'I see them grow and I see that I am still growing too. I see myself in them, good and bad. I love them, so I should love me too.'

In some instances, it may mean trimming away the extra

layer of expectations you've been taught to place on yourself. If you have a male partner, perhaps it's about increasing the expectations you have of them. 'I love my kids in the most incredible way,' wrote Esther in the survey. 'It really changed me for the better. However, I lost myself in it for years. I think about all the time I could have been building my career and I get regretful. I do wonder if it's more of a disappointment in my partner. I chose someone who saw me as an equal but somehow that didn't translate into childcare.'

In her book, Adrienne Rich addresses how the idea of motherhood is a conflicting one, which often straitjackets women. 'Throughout patriarchal mythology, dream-symbolism, theology, language, two ideas flow side by side: one, that the female body is impure, corrupt, the site of discharges, bleedings, dangerous to masculinity, a source of moral and physical contamination, "the devil's gateway,"' she writes.

'On the other hand, as mother, the woman is beneficent, sacred, pure, asexual, nourishing; and the physical potential for motherhood – that same body with its bleedings and mysteries – is her single destiny and justification in life. These two ideas have become deeply internalized in women, even in the most independent of us, those who seem to lead the freest lives.'

When we refer to patriarchal motherhood, what we are referring to is the extra burden mothers are made to carry, and the lack of support structurally and institutionally.

Although the domestic labour gap between men and women has narrowed, there is still an uneven balance in terms of who does what, ranging from feeding the kids (even when they are older) to who is the primary caregiver when things go wrong. As things stand, men generally gain status and rights as a result of being a father, and get to keep their careers, and their bodies are not altered by the process.

Women gain status as a result of being a mother (and before we scoff, consider the way women without children are treated because they haven't fulfilled their 'purpose'), but they have to lose a lot in order to get it. They are more exposed to unequal pay, they lose autonomy over their time and their bodies, their health is in the hands of a healthcare system that does not treat their lives equally, they do a fuckload of unpaid work and being pressured to compete with other mothers can be isolating.

In some cases, women have to switch to flexible working because of childcare. Given that such jobs often involve zero-hours contracts, this can affect their pension entitlements when they are older, leaving them financially worse-off. Although the decision may be made for the overall benefit of the family, and may be a choice a woman willingly takes, she will most likely end up more vulnerable and less financially protected as a result of that choice.

Some of these issues could be partly solved through the dismantling of patriarchal fatherhood, including using gender-neutral terms such as parental leave, allowing parents to decide for themselves how to split it. The UK is lagging far behind in this, compared to certain Scandinavian countries which have long been held as the gold standard in Europe. But there have recently been other European countries that have implemented far better policies than the UK, such as

SHE WANTED MORE

Germany, where fathers have the option to take up to thirty-six months of parental leave within the first three years of their child's life. This is partly aimed at getting more people back into the workforce, but the German government also recognises that it allows more involvement from the father, and that has a positive impact on child development.

Encouragingly, there has been a significant cultural shift around this too, as conversations around masculinity have evolved. Writing in *The Guardian*, evolutionary anthropologist Dr Anna Machin said that fatherhood has changed 'beyond recognition in the past 50 years'.

'Today, fathers no longer want to be limited to the role of family breadwinner and disciplinarian,' she wrote. 'They want to be true co-parents, providing nurture and care to their children. This change is due in part to the rise of two-earner households, reductions in hospital-based post-birth care and an absence of geographically close extended family, requiring dad to step in.'[28]

One thing that drives author and journalist Lotte Jeffs mad is the constant advertising and references directed at mums that deepen the gender role divide. Jeffs identifies as non-binary and has written books about queer parenting. They have a child with their wife Jenny, via an anonymous donor, after wanting to be a parent from a young age, and said that parenting is the 'best thing I've ever done.'

The queer community is a great one to learn from around parenting, partly because they have to be intentional, rather than just absorbing pre-existing ideas, and partly because there is more fluidity around gender roles. 'That kind of targeted advertising ... it's as though mums are the only ones that have any responsibility for children in any respect,' Lotte said. 'E.g. "here's something for the summer holidays for you to entertain your kids." Like, why is it just mums? Why can't it just be parents? It excludes all the amazing dads out there – gay or straight – and perpetuates this narrative that women are the only primary caregivers to their children.'

For some people, motherhood is such a fundamental part of their identity that the idea of questioning it can seem terrifying. 'When we think of the hardships within the realm of motherhood, we think of the guilt, the physical burdens, the emotional taxation, the isolation, the rage,' wrote Alexandra D'amour in her motherhood newsletter *On Our Moon*. 'Having nowhere to direct blame, we point to ourselves (or worse, each other), and not the social (patriarchal) contracts we unknowingly sign when we become mothers.'

Women are waking up to the idea that they can love being mothers, *and* they change what motherhood means to them too. This allows us to reimagine a world for so many, including women who might not fit the template of what we've been told mothering should look like.

Having seen women who have children with male partners they've settled with, who are now leading complicated and sometimes stagnant lives as a consequence, I wonder if having an honest and positive conversation about alternative identities could lead to different decision-making. Of course, some people may still decide that a mediocre relationship is better than being a single parent, but I also feel that making alternate ways of parenting more visible (and validating them to sit alongside partnered parenting) could give women more freedom and options.

* * *

I know two people who chose to parent solo from the very beginning, and one of those is my friend and agent Rowan Lawton, who chose to have her child via a donor.

While I'm cautious about extrapolating the experiences of those closest to me and inflating them into a universal truth, Rowan's story was one of the very few that showed me how motherhood could be attained outside the usual 2.4 children template. She decided in her mid-thirties that she didn't want to wait to meet a partner in order to have a child, and after talking to her family about how it might work and the help that she'd need, she went ahead and had her daughter Kit. At the time I hadn't made my mind up about having children, and it was helpful to see the possibilities and how things could work differently.

'Our bond feels very special as a unit of two,' Rowan told me, 'and we can really suit ourselves, whether that's dancing around the kitchen on a Friday night with our "special" drinks and snacks, or travelling on quite grown-up trips and outings when we can be totally present with each other and have fun in non-child-centred environments or just lie next to each other reading our books for an hour (which suits me down to the ground ... soft play mum I am not).

'I love how close Kit is to her grandparents and my brother and his family. I think I also have an even closer relationship with my parents than I might otherwise as we're so involved in each other's day-to-day lives because of how much support they give us. There are definitely challenging moments – sometimes practical, sometimes emotional. Practically, family life on a single income with a full-time job and sole responsibility for all the work to be done at home too is tiring to say the least. Emotionally, I am sometimes caught unawares by a sense of our difference, particularly when we're in traditional family settings, like, say, a family group holiday or events.'

I think it can be helpful for people with children to see how other parents in different circumstances are doing it, in order to find hope or perhaps a solution to their own situation. One of the most inspiring stories I came across recently was that of Shannon Foote, who was a single mother of four, and after the breakup of her relationship, decided to co-parent with her best friend Cheyanne, who has two children. She regularly posts videos on TikTok titled 'two single moms raising 6 kids' and it's an insight into how they support each other. They share chores, and when one of them is sick, the other takes care of all the children.

Amid the men sourly saying 'two moms who couldn't keep a man', a mother commented on one of their posts: 'I did this with one of my best friends for a few years and it was amazing! We took turns cooking without asking each other whose turn it should be. Picked up each other's kids after school or took them to school rehearsals . . . it was so seamless too. No reminders, no asking. Probably one of the best partnerships I've ever had and, more importantly, the kids were happy.'

Another person who inspired me around the same time as

SHE WANTED MORE

Rowan had her daughter was the author Laura Jane Williams, who did single adoption. Laura said the idea was planted when she was working at a Toys R Us while at university. 'One day, I tried to talk to a girl sitting in a trolley as her grown-up browsed. It turns out the woman was her foster carer, and she said the child was mute with everyone except her sister – but her sister was in another foster placement. From that moment on children in care, and looking at how to take a child out of the care system, became a "real" thing that made sense to me.

'I readily accepted that my child would not be grown in my tummy, and that my child would be one who needed a mummy but didn't have one – for whatever reason. This was compounded by working as a nanny, where I fell so utterly in love with my charges that my heart understood biology is irrelevant. By the time I was thirty I'd achieved my dream of being published, but remember coming home from my second book launch and just sobbing because I wasn't coming home to kids upstairs in bed. The achievement of my work didn't feel like enough.'

Laura did a ton of research and talked to her parents about supporting her. She quit London for Derbyshire, where property is cheaper and she was able to buy a house. Her paperwork took a long time to get approved, but after it was, it was only a matter of weeks before she met her son. 'I feel strongly that adoption shouldn't be an insurance policy,' she said. 'The whole 'Oh, if I can't get pregnant I'll just adopt!' drives me crazy. It should be an eyes-wide-open decision. You can't resent this person for continuing to need you: spontaneous nights out are off the agenda for a long time, so is decent sleep. But what I will say is that being a solo adopter is the most rewarding, sublimely dedicated act of devotion I have ever experienced, and I love harder and deeper than I ever thought possible.'

I am fascinated by the type of motherhood that pushes beyond the societal norm, because of how much work a person needs to do in order to figure themselves out as a mother. I spoke to Ranji Thangiah, the creator of a Sri Lankan food-themed Substack called *Tooting Mama*, who adopted when she was forty-two (thirteen years ago). She and her husband tried to go down the IVF route, but it was unsuccessful and triggered a deep depression in Ranji. After a natural pregnancy that sadly miscarried, she allowed herself to grieve and then asked herself the question: *do I still want a family?* Her South Asian husband had been adopted by a white family and so adoption felt like a natural progression in their journey.

'Motherhood was thrust on me and the first few months were tough,' she told me. 'Initially, the children rejected me. My kids had a foster mum with whom they were very happy, and all they wanted was a dad. They got a dad who just happened to come with a mum who they didn't want. I had to build trust and earn their love, and respect. I had to keep loving kids who let out their trauma by raging at me.

'But I just had to show up, day after day, and be Mum. I remember keeping notes of the small gestures the kids did, like wanting to brush my hair, giving me a flower, and drawing me a picture. That's when I knew I was breaking through. I took on the role of silly mum. I taught them my party trick – burping on demand – which they loved!'

SHE WANTED MORE

Ranji's identity shifted over time. At first she thought she had to give up everything to be their mother, and then realised that wasn't the case. 'I had to find ways to allow the two identities to co-exist. I managed to eke out ways to reclaim bits of myself. Writing became important. It helped me to understand my feelings, and my kids' feelings, and process the craziness of this new life.

'As someone who has grown up in a time where it was the status quo for a woman to give up her dreams for her children, and lives in a time where women are trying to make their dreams co-exist alongside their children, I am eager to see how this shift will ripple through the current generations of 30–40-something women.'

* * *

Perhaps it is the cleansing effect of peri-menopause and menopause, but women in their forties, fifties and beyond are already redesigning what motherhood looks like for them. For many, it looks like retaining the love, intensity and joy their children give them, while also reconnecting to themselves.

One of the biggest catalysts for this is the fact that women are having children at a later age than they used to. According to the Office for National Statistics, girls in England and Wales turning eighteen in 2025 are more likely to have one child by the age of thirty-five, whereas their mothers' generation would have had their first child by thirty-one.[29] For women of my mother's generation, this would have been roughly twenty-six years old – my mother was twenty-five when she gave birth to my sister.

If motherhood is taking place slightly later than it used to, then the effect of peri-menopause and menopause (the biggest life shift for cisgender women since puberty) will impact your children, and your identity as a mother at a different stage from the one older women experienced. For instance, I was a teenager when my mother was likely experiencing peri-menopause, while now, it stands to reason that peri-menopause will be hitting women when their children are younger.

Although menopause is still largely described as a negative experience for women, a growing number of women do speak of it as a major clarifier in terms of having less capacity to do things for others.

Even having access to knowledge around these hormonal shifts is a marked change from my mother's generation, who had little understanding of them, and often felt alone in their experiences. It may have a positive impact on parenting, both for boys – in terms of understanding that women are not there to endlessly serve them – and for girls, in terms of knowing their value exists beyond doing things for others.

This biological shift helps to push through the realisation that you do not need to do everything, and be everything, for your child. That your child actually learns from many different people, and from being in many different places. I loved what Bozoma Saint John had to say about it on the podcast *The Mama's Den*. 'I wasn't put here to manage her. I was put here to help guide her in her own journey. I'm not responsible for every single little thing that she's supposed to learn.'

There is a lot to consider, then, when it comes to figuring out your identity as a mother.

SHE WANTED MORE

I'll close this chapter with one of my favourite quotes from Ellora, who took part in the survey, which I think sums this up. 'I'm not sure if we have a purpose,' she wrote, 'but if we do, it is to love and to learn. I haven't experienced this love in any other relationships, but that doesn't mean I think my child-free friends aren't living fulfilling lives; indeed they're more fulfilled than I am. It's just I needed to have had children who I've loved unconditionally to learn this lesson. There are other ways to learn it, I'm sure.'

CHAPTER SEVEN

OTHERHOOD: THE SHIFT IN IDENTITY AROUND NOT BEING A PARENT

It took me a very long time to learn that although mainstream society defines a woman by her status as a mother or not, it is not always a binary choice or a linear journey. On a childfree/childless spectrum, where one end is something so sad it almost tears a person apart, and at the other end there is peace and clarity, there is a lot of middle which is not always about choice, but rather circumstance. It is a complicated, isolating identity. Therefore, one of the most beautiful shifts in the last few years has been the creation of community for these women, wherever they sit on the scale.

One of the biggest advocates is Jody Day, founder of Gateway Women, an advocacy group for women who don't have children. Although she now lives in rural Ireland, Jody grew up in a working-class family in England.

Talking about her journey, she said: 'Having children was

not a choice for me, but even the word "choice" is complex as I was sure I didn't want children until I'd been married (to my first husband) for a few years. Having been part of his large, loving family, I decided at twenty-nine that I *did* want to have children. However, once we started trying for a baby, I then struggled with unexplained infertility, which was a factor in the breakdown of my marriage at thirty-eight.

'We'd been together sixteen years by the time we split in my late thirties, but fuelled by babymania, I shot out of that marriage like a cannonball and into the then new world of internet dating. I was determined to meet someone else and do IVF, completely unaware of the likelihood of it working for me (somewhere between 1–5%), and also that I was in no fit shape emotionally to be dating. Unsurprisingly, I didn't meet the right person, so at that point, I was "childless by circumstance".

'And then, as a single, childless woman in my forties, I grieved both of those identities deeply, before arriving at a place of peace by the end of my forties. In my fifties, I came to the realisation that I probably felt as at peace with my childlessness as if I had chosen it (although I can never be 100% sure as I don't get to live both lives), so now, in my sixties, in a way I'm childfree again. This is why for me, the idea that childlessness or childfree is a fixed identity, a binary, seems inadequate.'

Pulling apart the strand of storytelling around the childfree/childless identity is important for a few reasons.

If motherhood had been presented as a choice, rather than something non-negotiable, to the women of my mother's generation, I believe there would be fewer adults impacted by the trauma of having a negligent or abusive parent. I am not making excuses for anyone who damages their child in this way, but it stands to reason that there may be a causal link between someone never wanting to be a parent but having children anyway, because it was expected at the time, and this kind of behaviour.

If we can wrap our heads around concepts like people having different professions, hobbies and preferences, as well as understanding neuro-divergency, then we should be able to comprehend that perhaps not everyone wants to be or can be a parent.

'I know having kids would have been the wrong decision for me,' wrote Helena in the survey. 'I'd rather risk regret not having kids than regret fucking up my kids' life. I feel like I escape the judgement part in some way because people perceive me as someone who's been focusing on her education and career but think that one day I'll still pursue a nuclear family, just maybe later than average. But in reality I don't plan to, and when people find out, judgements and comments become more common. I hate that I'm still seen as a future mother first, even when it's clear that my priorities never lay there and even when I clarify that it never will.'

For women who want children but are unable to have them – either due to circumstance or fertility reasons – there has to be some hope, some resolution at the end of their journey. A counter-narrative could help enormously – that there is purpose and meaning beyond having children. You can hold sadness and grief around it, *and* you can be held by a society that doesn't make you feel excluded.

'I feel like a failure after two pregnancy losses,' wrote Ramona in the survey. 'People around me and the world in general is geared towards women who have children. There is very little to no support for those that have tried and still don't have them. It's like I don't exist or can't do anything meaningful with my life. If we don't have children I'm confident I will still be an actual person who exists and should be valued.'

It took grief for me to learn how unoriginal people are when expressing an opinion about things they can't comprehend, and it took being childfree for the lesson to be underlined. If you tell people you don't want children, so many say things like:

- You'll never know a love like it
- Who will look after you when you are older?
- It's selfish not to have children
- You don't want to regret not having them

Then it took me turning forty to realise how unimaginably cruel it would be to say any of these things to someone who wants children but is struggling to conceive or find a partner to have a child with.

Normalise not having a fucking opinion on what someone else does with their body. Kids are a joy and a wonder and I get that. But given that we aren't in any danger of dying out as a species, I think it's okay to take a breath and let people live their lives the way they want to – because you don't know who you are going to harm by pushing this 'when are you having kids?' line of questioning.

SHE WANTED MORE

'I started a new job recently,' Tini wrote in the survey, 'and the number of people that asked whether I had children was shocking. Like "'hi, we've just met, can I ask you something that will touch on an incredibly sensitive theme, thanks.'"

Also, normalise questioning these tropes.

The whole 'who will look after you when you're older?' mindset is partly what has led to the misery of the sandwich generation, aka the current generation of fifty-somethings who have the stress of looking after their own kids as well as their elderly parents and have gained all manner of health issues from carrying this double burden.[30]

Even if someone has chosen to be childfree out of choice, as I have, it doesn't necessarily mean we hate children, or that we don't value our ability to nurture. And I refer to the word 'nurture' in its truest sense – not running around after people and doing domestic labour but helping to raise and protect younglings in a wide variety of ways, from what we teach them to the experiences we share with them. With regard to my niece Leela, I consider it my responsibility to help her understand the world, as well as taking her on little trips to art galleries and going for brunch. Am I going to be the one fetching her snacks and doing her laundry? Hell no. But there are other parts of her life that I want to be part of, that I feel I can help with.

While the global north has shifted the idea of parenting to nuclear families, the idea of collectively raising children has always resonated strongly with me because that's how it's often done in India. Even more broadly, I know plenty of people who've been raised by aunts, uncles, grandparents and family friends because their parents did not have the capacity or were no longer around, and it feels to me like a richer society for it.

Even if we have no wish to nurture at all, there should be better inclusion in society for people who don't have children. In the survey, 44% of childfree women said they felt socially excluded because of it. You shouldn't have to earn your place in society based on your proximity to procreation.

'It seems like we went from the media/society stigmatising childfree women as being "less than" or figures to be pitied, to governments panicking that more people are choosing to be childfree,' wrote Rina in the survey, referring to the 2024 statistics that birth rates in the UK were decreasing. 'That makes me mad because there isn't enough support from the government or society to help with the raising of said children. And also because it's made out that we have a moral obligation to have kids.

'I am in a phase of life where I'm finding it hard to continue friendships with my friends who do have kids, and it's a difficult one to navigate. I understand that my friends have new priorities, but I also don't want to spend big chunks of my weekends doing child-friendly activities all the time. Maybe it's the way I was socialised and it's my own baggage from that, but I do feel judged by new people I meet when they find out I'm childfree. Like they think I'm a complete weirdo for making that choice.'

Although the percentage of women in their forties and older who don't have children is much smaller than the number of women who do have children, that number is growing.

SHE WANTED MORE

According to a 2023 report by the Pew Research Centre, 47% of US adults younger than fifty said they were unlikely to have children.[31] The fertility rate in the US has reached an all-time low, as it has in the UK. That isn't just because people are choosing not to have children – other reasons include not finding a partner, not being able to afford to have children, and fertility issues.

We have to talk about this stuff. The belief that it's a woman's purpose to have children is so pervasive and strong that, even if you think you are immune to being defined by it, it has a way of insidiously sliding under your skin when you're in your forties. As someone who doesn't have children, I have spent the last year feeling disorientated around my sense of purpose. That is partly because most of my contemporaries have children, and there is no road-mapping for what purpose looks like as a childfree 45-year-old woman. Life has its challenges, but I'm mostly doing what I love, with people I love, and it feels... strange.

When Jody Day starting writing about this back in 2011, it was born from a desire to change the perception of women without children, and to ensure their voices mattered. 'Society continues to see women without children as a social problem to be fixed, or some kind of trendy lifestyle issue,' she said. 'Women without children... contribute hugely to our families, communities and wider society, not least of all through the taxes we pay to support the civic society and infrastructure for other people's children.' (When she said this last part, the outrage I felt at the realisation of it made me yell, 'OH MY GOD, WE DO!!')

'We are not anti-mothers or anti-children, but mothers are the only women that patriarchy gives status to. Hence the "As a mother..." statements that can be used to endorse just about anything. Can you imagine a politician saying "As a childless/childfree woman...." No, women without children are not considered to be fully mature adults and thus not worth listening to.'

The perceived immaturity of childfree people has always struck me as odd, given that we have to plan for our future because there is no safety net, and often, in the case of single folk, manage all our life admin alone, from paying bills to doing household chores. And yet this mindset persists – that we have no say in the future of our world because we don't have children. And this idea has been weaponised by influential people over the years.

When I spoke to Sari Botton about this, she said: 'I must admit that as a childless woman, I struggle with this too. I'm finding that being sixty now, and having friends who are now becoming grandparents, it's harder still. This is largely a problem of projection, taking on an old, patriarchal view of what gives a woman worth, even if I don't intellectually believe it. Sometimes, even when it's what you want, it can be emotionally challenging to live counter to your culture. But in my bones I know not being a mother is right for me.'

Having people reaffirm that a sense of purpose can exist beyond children, therefore, helps. 'In her Oldster Magazine Questionnaire,' Sari added, 'author Elizabeth Gilbert wrote about bravely bucking what she was told. She wrote: "I had been taught by my family and culture that there is nothing more tragic than a single, childless, middle-aged woman. But as someone who has now been twice-divorced and once widowed, I am amazed by how great it is to be on my own, to live alone, to travel alone, to chart my own course in life without having to run it by anyone. It's the fucking bomb.'"

In the last few years, I've had to deconstruct my decision-making around having children. Some people, for instance, know they don't want them from a young age, while it's a bit more complicated for me. In the Pew report, older respondents who didn't have children said it 'just didn't happen' for them, while 57% of younger cohorts said they actively didn't want them, and I definitely identify with the former.

To highlight the nuance of it, allow me to share something very personal, which I have never told a single soul.

* * *

Let me tell you about the child I didn't have. Her name was Aroha, and she was meant to be the emblem of mine and Rob's love for each other. On the rare occasions I think of her, I close my eyes and I can see the thickness of her dark curls, I imagine whether she would have had my eyes – a greenish blue, or Rob's – deep blue. I don't think about her often, or indeed too much, but it isn't always the sorrowful, desperate thing you might imagine it to be. She never existed, not in the way it counts, and my body remains unchanged by her.

I just know there was a moment in time when she was a possibility, and I remember the day that door closed forever, as Rob and I stood opposite each other in a carpeted room in The Priory where he was an inpatient. When we knew we would not be able to have children together. His addiction was too strong, and the risk of bringing a life into that was something we could never, would never, have subjected a child to.

I might not know what it is like to be a mother, but I know I felt enough love for that could-be child that if I couldn't guarantee she would have a safe life, a good life from the very beginning, it wouldn't be right. It couldn't just be 'because I wanted it'. It had to be what was best for her. And that love was not nothing.

* * *

As a child, the idea of playing mummies with dolls never really appealed to me. Nevertheless, as I grew older, I always assumed I would get married one day and have children, but there was never a specific desire or need to become a mother. The only time I was aware of my desire was when Priya and her first husband talked about not wanting to have children (something that obviously changed for my sister along the way). Unlike them, I knew I did want children. When I met Rob, we talked about kids very early on in our relationship, when he informed me that we would be having beautiful 'international beige babies', and I wove it into the cloak of love I wrapped around us.

We never actively tried to have children because his health got worse and worse; it didn't feel like the right time. Until time stopped altogether.

After he passed, it was something I came back to briefly two years later when I was thirty-six, and possibly in the midst of a mad rush of hormones. I was walking down a road in Shillong in India while on holiday with my parents, and saw a gang of little girls just being joyful and laughing. I felt a tug, a powerful one, pulling me towards motherhood. Around that time, I remember talking to Laura Jane Williams about her plan to adopt as a single mother and felt inspired by her determination.

But when those hormones passed, I forgot about adopting. It merely slid down a crack somewhere, like a melted ice cream. And I was sure that the desire to parent should be something that is part of your core, not something that flits in and out of your consciousness. At the very least, you *remember* it's something you want to do.

Something that makes your late thirties unnecessarily unpleasant is that it feels as if time is running out in a number of ways. Having children biologically is a part of that and, unless you are privileged enough to be able to afford egg freezing or alternate ways of conceiving, it puts a lot of pressure on meeting someone and the question of having children. After the 'forgetting about adoption' period, I started to wonder for the first time – do I *want* to be a parent, or is it that I feel pressured to be? And when did I first realise I wanted children? Was it before Rob or during? And did I actually *want* children or did it just feel like a thing you did, like all the other choices on the relationship escalator? Meet someone, start dating, move in together, get engaged, get married, have kids, etc.?

Eventually I realised that I didn't want children. That I had never, not once, thought about *actual* motherhood and what it was like to raise a child – only that it was 'something you did'. Whichever part of me did want them died with Rob. Losing him almost destroyed me, and I didn't have the capacity to potentially risk losing a child. I had earned the right to say that. But fuck me, try vocalising that to people who kept insisting otherwise.

Turning forty was a blessed relief, not only because it crystallised the kids thing for me into a definitive 'no', but because people assumed I was too old anyway, and they stopped saying things like 'it might still happen', and 'you might change your mind' and 'no one is ever ready'.

I have also realised how no one benefits if we treat the topic of children from a defensive position. There is space for women to express how deeply satisfying and complex it is to be a parent, and there should be space to express how wonderful it is to not be one. And there absolutely should be space for the grief of those who feel a sense of loss within that identity. All these things can co-exist, and we should take a moment to realise that even being able to debate things like identity and motherhood is a vast improvement on what our own mothers dealt with.

'We didn't even question whether or not we wanted to be parents,' my mother said to me. 'We just did it.' There was no alternative for women of her generation, and I thank the universe every day that there are alternatives for mine.

While my journey is as much about circumstance as it is about choice, I feel sure that I would not have been the mother my mother is. I don't think, even now, I am capable of that kind of softness. Although everyone is quick to tell me that I am, I know in my bones and my heart that, while my love for Aroha exists, just as quickly I release it into the atmosphere to set her soul free – to travel onwards to someone, somewhere, so that it doesn't bind me, or her, so that both of us can journey onwards to where we should be, instead of where we might have been.

* * *

When I was young, a woman without children was always spoken about as if she was a malfunctioning toy. Growing up in India, there was a woman in our cul-de-sac who didn't have children, and we were terrified when our ball landed in her garden because the rumour was that she wouldn't give it back. Retrospectively, she was probably sick of little shits kicking a ball at her window, and she did give us the ball back if we asked nicely, but at the time, she was talked about as a semi-mythical, malignant person who apparently wished us harm. Even adults spoke about her with a raised eyebrow – *she never says hello, she's a strange woman.*

Back then the lesson was simple – if you don't have children and you aren't married, there must be something wrong with you. Which also implied the opposite – if you're married and have children, then your life must be sorted. And no one benefits from that kind of clumsy logic, which creates harmful stereotypes on both sides.

The stereotype of a woman without children is someone who is fundamentally alone, and therefore unhappy. It destabilises friendships in your thirties, especially if your friends are having children and you're not. It's something

I experienced, and it's still something I see in agony aunt columns, along the lines of 'all my friends are having children and they don't have time for me anymore'.

If you're a parent, I understand that such complaints sound petulant. Especially if you're trying your best to survive while raising a child, with all the associated delights of sleep deprivation and a lighter bank balance. However, it speaks to the growing pains people have to experience in order to understand the fundamentals about friendships, particularly as we get older. They must be intentional, and having new people in our lives who reflect where we are at, not just where we have been, is vital in order to feel contentment.

I spent several years feeling unhappy and lonely because I didn't see my friends as much, and then got deeply resentful at always having to work around them, or having to spend our rare catch-up times with their kids in tow, until I realised that something had to change. It wasn't about being right or wrong. It was a case of acknowledging that we were simply at different stages of our lives and that I needed to find some childfree friends.

Switching that intention was critical because it made me become proactive about making new friends, which was a muscle that had atrophied. Usually we make friends as a natural response to the environment we are in, whether that is school, university, or the workplace. When I found myself working as a 37-year-old freelancer, with no clear way of meeting new people and with old friends unavailable, I felt profoundly disconnected from society.

After quitting my job in 2018, I moved to a new area and

happened to join a new gym. I didn't realise that it was a community gym, which meant that people talked and knew each other, and slowly I got absorbed into the more social aspect of it. Part of that led to joining a powerlifting team that the head coach, Jack, ran out of the gym, along with his training partner Lindsay. Jack is a pied piper of lost souls, and he has played a pivotal role in creating a community of people who are searching for resonance and belonging. At first he would invite me to the team dinners, which I resisted, until I went along and found that I could make conversation with people I didn't know well.

That slowly led to making new friends, and one of the most enduring of these friendships has been Jack's wife Aga, who is one of the loves of my life, and who introduced me to grappling sports. My friendship with her – and others who have joined along the way – has helped me feel the delight I felt about friendships when I was a child, as well as the maturity to understand what it takes to power a friendship. To be happy for each other, to make plans, to show care.

My newer friendships enabled me to understand three things – that the expectations I had of my old friends were not realistic or fair; that friendship had to include reciprocity (not just one person making all the effort); and that showing up for each other mattered a lot. And by that, I don't just mean what we all did in our thirties – spending loads of money on each other or going to innumerable hen dos. I mean creating a real community – being there for each other when you need someone to come to your house and water your plants or feed your cat, thinking of each other and demonstrating it, understanding what is important to the other person, making new memories with each other. Not just having endless catch-ups about what is going wrong in each other's lives and thinking that is what constitutes friendship.

Being childfree is often seen as being 'less than', but I believe that it has made me more intentional about my life, and I don't feel as if I am on autopilot. And because I feel seen in my life, I don't feel the need to fight so hard for my existence to be validated. It isn't the utopia that people in childfree clap-back videos post about, and it isn't a sad little life either.

I love the freedom of being childfree: that my finances are my own, that I can have lots of sleep and I don't have to shelve my needs. I also know there is a real fear about what will happen when I am older. Not in a 'kids are my retirement plan' kind of way, but more just having someone who cares about me enough to make sure I'm alive and I'm okay. When I see, for instance, some of the adults in my life who are being taken care of by their children financially, there is an 'oh fuck' moment of anxiety about what will happen to me.

But I also know that all of this is still not enough to make me want to have children, not just because I don't want them but because I have seen enough elderly parents still having to take care of their grown-up children, and they are *tired*. There's no guarantee parenting will yield what you need.

Although it is relatively uncharted territory, I feel that the path for old age needs to be a radical one, built on community and extending beyond relying on adult children. Whether it's discussing setting up a commune, or living in houses near our friends and family, there are ways in which we can all look after each other in our old age, rather than placing the burden on any one person. Even if you have children, this extended network of peers and friends feels important. Having seen the difference among my parents' generation that friendship can make to the vitality they feel in their life, it is something that should be prioritised just as much as our pensions or any other long-term planning. The safety net of community and friendship allows people to leave marriages when they are older and still have full, loving lives.

In 2014, Jody Day was one of four people who set up Ageing Without Children, an organisation that has gone on to become a UK charity, but that apparently struggled to secure funding despite the increase in people over sixty-five without adult children. In the present day, she has focused on her own tiny rural Irish community and is building a group called Alterkin, which is a community of care for those ageing without children. 'The appetite for "Alternative Kinship Circles" (which is what my word Alterkin is short for) is huge,' she said, 'and not just limited to non-parents, but those from other marginalised communities (such as LGBGT+) who are the most receptive to and experienced with the concepts of communities of care.'

In a 2023 interview with Alison Palmer, founder of the Crones, Hags & Elder Wise Women of Power Summit, Jody said: 'I already know probably about ten childless women in the Irish county that I live in, County Cork, and I've been running a "Gathering" (like a meetup) for them for a couple of years now.

'So let's imagine, in twenty years' time, some of those relationships have developed in certain ways . . . I love the idea that there would be a group of people locally who knew me, who had invested in a relationship with me over time, and they could say, "Okay, I'll walk Jody's dog" and another might say, "Okay, I'll do the shopping", and another might say, "'I'll go and clean her house." And that there might be a group of people who could perhaps get involved, rather than all that care falling heavily on one person, when it's too much, on top of managing their own life and commitments. And I love the idea of having a sort of team around me who are doing it because they know me well, even perhaps love me, because we've spent years actively supporting each other with our lives.'

While my worries about growing older haven't entirely gone away, the diversity of thought, and stories about what life could look like, has expanded. In the same way as getting older doesn't have to equate to frailty, getting older doesn't necessarily equate to loneliness. If loneliness can exist among older people with children as well as people without, then perhaps the problem isn't whether or not we have kids. Perhaps it is how much we have been taught – or, rather, not taught – to prioritise friendships and community that exist beyond our dependants and partners.

This is something that the LGBTQ+ community understands out of necessity. Owing to a higher rate of ostracisation by their friends and/or family due to their sexuality, they create their own community that they refer to as 'the chosen family'. The richness of these bonds, the sense of taking care of each other, is beautiful to witness, and offers a lesson in how connection makes a life bloom.

It is something that everyone – queer or not – could learn from, because that sense of judgement doesn't seem to ease off as you get older. As Esther said in the survey: 'In my youth, people were judgmental about not having children, and now as I approach my sixties this is apparent amongst the senior ladies, e.g. not having grandchildren. But between my forties and late fifties, people were envious of my decision to not have children. Either way, I still have no regrets about not having children.'

* * *

While writing this chapter, I wanted to take particular care with the community of people who are childfree not by choice. Although I don't have the data, I feel that they may account for a bigger percentage of childfree women than we realise. The most important thing for them to know is that it is possible to hold that sadness and still create new moments of joy, and that there is life and purpose after grief.

Some of the many people who fit this bracket, who wrote in for the survey, said they allowed themselves to grieve, and found things like creative pursuits, or had sought out therapy. Others were planning adventures and holidays, developing hobbies and 'trying to enjoy the freedom with feeling guilty'. One woman said that being childless helped her to leave her marriage, while another said they gave themselves a lot of time to adjust their identity, adding: 'Infertility loss hits hard and often. But I'm also keenly aware that I've become kinda awesome without kids so I do have positive and revelatory moments as well.'

Wherever we sit on this particular spectrum – childfree by choice, not by choice, or as a parent – certain truths apply. The more I experience life, the more convinced I am that we all need each other, and operating in silos won't help anyone. I need other childfree people in my life, but I have no desire to live in segregation with them alone. As much as I need resonance, I also need to live in a world with hope, and the stories my parent friends tell about their kids – the funny, weird, sweet little things they say, the stories that show their purity and kindness – give me that. They and Leela show me that even when my edges grow worn, and my heart feels heavy, and I think I've seen it all, something new can grow, and that fills my world with delight.

CHAPTER EIGHT

DATING, EXPECTATIONS AND THE JOOP-SCENTED REALITY

Dating in my forties is wildly different to how it was in my twenties and thirties, and for anyone talking about how much harder it is, I need you to know this truth: there is no stage in your life when dating is framed as being fun or empowering for a woman. It's generally viewed as a means to an end.

The only time it ever seemed cool or exciting was when I was a teenager – in other words, a child. And that was mainly because, as a brown teenager, dating was off-limits and therefore enormously alluring.

Once you realise that dating has always been seen as a means of escaping from your single life, it allows you to do two things. First, to consider whether your single life is something you really want to escape from. (A number of women in their forties, such as myself, who have been through significant life stages such as marriage, have actually created a peaceful life that runs counter to the chaos a relationship can sometimes bring.) Second, to reposition dating as something that works for you and is fun, rather than a gladiatorial slog. When we reduce dating to the simplicity of 'I'd like to have a nice conversation with someone and see if there is a connection', it removes a lot of the weight and expectation we normally attach to it.

I understand that it may sound impossible. Currently, dating is going through a crisis because of the mental wear and tear of apps, and the increasing social disconnection between people in general – leading to a collective sense of malaise and disillusionment. In your twenties, it is a fraught business that hinges around you finding a life partner. In your thirties it becomes even more frantic, and in your forties you're told that you should have made more of an effort when you were younger, because now you will be saddled with the social rejects no one else wanted.

While it may be a blessed relief to be in a monogamous relationship where you never again have to talk about how many people are in your family, there is also a heavier responsibility that comes with your life being anchored to one other person. Dating can be hard because people are hard, but it can also be fun and light. The dates I have enjoyed the most have been the ones with good chat and clear communication, regardless of how they ended. The ones I have enjoyed the least were when I was looking to the other person to fill a void, or vice versa.

Dating in my forties is a neutral concept for me. I'd love

to meet someone long-term, but I don't go into a date expecting or wanting that. I initially reduce it to just wanting to make a beautiful connection with someone. It is easier for me because I don't want children, but if you do, it is still important to start with lightness and fun while keeping your intentions in mind, to feed that spark with enough oxygen for it to catch light.

Dating is also easier for me now because if I am not enjoying myself, or I get a weird vibe, I don't second-guess that or hope it will get better. I just finish my drink and leave. This includes one guy who I'm pretty sure was doing coke outside the pub before we were due to meet. It's different to being unsure about whether or not I like someone – that feels like a tug in the gut which everyone recognises.

I also put care and love into my body before going on a date and that has nothing to do with the person I am meeting. I take my time slowly while getting ready, rub orange and cedar oil into my skin, pick an outfit that makes me feel good, listen to music that soothes me. It feels like self-worship. And by the time I am finished, I am whole.

* * *

Given current life expectancies, in general ageing terms, the 'third act' refers to people from the age of sixty. It follows that our forties and fifties are the second act, and everything that precedes them is the first.

In a three-act play, the second act tends to be referred to as 'the rising action', which feels appropriate when discussing the expansion and change for women around dating. It is the moment when the main character faces the forces that pull at them, that cause conflict, and – through one crisis or another – they have to dig deep to find their strength, heart and inner growth. By the time we reach the third act, there is a climax (pun fully intended), and then, a sense of resolution. But that's not the story we are told in society.

A woman over forty is told that the dating pool is very small, and you don't have the luxury of being picky. We have a shorthand, thanks to the patriarchy, which says that younger women are more desirable than older women, and this pits women against each other. If you are a woman over forty who wants to date or have sex, there is a sense that you must be desperate, and happy to accept anything. 'Who would want you anyway? Too many owners,' a troll said on my TikTok about a date that had gone wrong.

People will say, 'Oh, this is what dating as an older person is like', as if our youth was filled with beautiful people who had no emotional issues, and we could just pluck who we wanted off the vine, like grapes in the garden of Dionysus. I'm sorry, what? Was it just me then, on those interminable nights spent trying to find The One, only to find The Someone with way too much hair gel and a faint whiff of Joop?

It's interesting because the first act – particularly when it comes to dating – tends to be unsatisfying, unless you married your childhood or university sweetheart. You are told that youth is everything only when you have passed the point of youthfulness. While you are still in it, it never feels like power. Although I enjoyed the messiness of my twenties, which felt intense and steeped in bad decision-making and cheap rum, at the time it mostly felt neurotic and filled with the hunger of wanting to be loved, but never quite feeling sated.

The second act, for me, has been the unlearning of that, and the realisation that I need to pursue power from within. Understanding why I've been taught certain things about men and women – especially ideas around purity and desire – and who benefits from it has been key to rewriting what I know. As always, vocabulary offers proof of the imbalance. While there is a negative word for an older woman who dates younger men – a cougar – there is no counterpart for men who date younger women. They are just men who date women. Similarly, there are positive words for an older man who is attractive – silver fox, zaddy – but there is no equivalent for an older woman. Even the queer interpretation of the word 'mother' (you will have heard it initially in drag culture) is used to describe a woman within the context of reverence, and the leadership she provides; not necessarily as someone who is desirable.

The second act has also ushered in the realisation that there is no word that will validate or summarise the desirability of midlife women because we don't need the approval of others, and certainly not that of men. It's nice to have, but it no longer defines us – that is simply not where we draw strength, wisdom and fulfilment from.

At present, there is a conversation raging around the term 'heterofatalism', coined by sexuality scholar Asa Seresin, which is used to describe Gen Z and younger millennial heterosexual women who no longer date men because of their consistently negative experiences in the dating world. 'It's hard to be positive about our relationships with men when it feels like we're losing the ability to coexist with them,' wrote Olivia Petter, one of the leading writers about the thirty-something single female experience, in *The Times*. But, Petter observed, there is a danger of it being a self-fulfilling prophecy, adding that listening to each other's stories of misery leads to a sense of dread and futility. I agree.

Although for hetero women, it is easy to cast men as the focal point of all their problems, it is hard not to see it as a doom spiral. This isn't to let men off from taking responsibility for how they behave in groups to looking after each other and themselves – but they do have the capacity to learn and be different. While I realise I am one of the lucky ones, I have to look no further for proof that men can be honourable than my own father.

Unlike the stereotype of South Asian dads, my father has never been the oppressive patriarch in our family. He never yells, has never once forced his idea of what women should be on myself or my sister. I'm pretty sure he never read a parenting book, but he knew from the moment we were born that he would be a different kind of father to us both. He has taught us that it is wholly possible to convey strength and softness, and that a man doesn't need to extract his power by subtracting a woman's.

When I talked to my mother about who was her biggest support while she was raising me as a baby, she cited him. I was taken aback because I didn't know he was all that involved. I just assumed he'd left it to her. 'Dad was not like the average man,' she said, 'because he was going through hell himself. He was studying for his surgeon's exams. He was working sixty, seventy hours a week, and yet he did his bit. He would change your nappy, take you to the babyminder's. He was the most understanding husband I could have had.'

His level of participation would be considered the basic minimum now; but then, it wasn't. No one is perfect, and of course he has his flaws like the rest of us, but he reminds me that men can change their behaviour, and who they are is not fixed.

Although single women in their forties and fifties who are divorced, or have never been married, are increasingly choosing to stay single, compared with previous generations, I don't think that's just because of pessimism about men. It feels more neutral than that; most likely because the pressure to get married and have babies is less intense – either because you've already done that, or because you haven't done it and aren't bothered.

Based on my own experience, and other women I have talked to, female expectations are higher than they used to be, and we are no longer lowering them for the sake of being in a relationship. While this may seem similar to heterofatalism, the tone feels less 'men are shit' and more 'these are my standards, and if you can meet them, great, and if not, we'll have to part ways.'

I talked to my friend Shannon Murray, disability activist and actor, about this. Although she is Gen X, while I am an elder millennial, her experience has been very similar to mine. One of our favourite things to do is to send each other voice notes about our escapades. 'My approach to dating has been more intentional,' she told me. 'I put up with less bullshit and flakiness, and I'm quicker to delete and move on. God knows I wasted my twenties and thirties ruminating on countless unreliable and inconsistent men. In the last few years, my attitude is that I'm down for fun, short-term, respectful connections, provided both parties are open and clear about their intentions.

'I'd like a partner in my life but my standards are higher and I won't stand for the fuckery my younger self accepted. I'm very aware how strong I am and I need someone who can match that, who has shoulders broad enough for me to occasionally lean on, and I've yet to find that in a man. I bring a lot and if you're not bringing it too then why would I waste my energy, share my bed and give up wardrobe space? In the meantime, I'm doing the kind of dating I dreamt of in my twenties but didn't have the tools, confidence or wisdom to navigate.'

'Women raising their standards' is something that has been mentioned in relation to aspects of the 'male loneliness epidemic'. This 'epidemic' exists for a number of reasons, one of which was referenced in *Psychology Today* by Gregory Matos in 2022.[32] Although the term has now entered main-stream vocabulary, Matos' article was one of the first to address it in the context of dating. He argued that men's reluctance to bridge the deficit between women's relationship expectations being higher, and them being used to meeting very low standards, was a contributing factor. However, it is important to note that the loneliness epidemic isn't just male – it affects women too, and according to some studies, at a higher rate, linking back to the lack of social connection mentioned earlier.[33]

SHE WANTED MORE

The second reason women stay single as they get older is the re-prioritisation of joy, hobbies and friendship, so that they lead relatively full lives, filled with possibilities. They are no longer looking to a partner for a sense of purpose, nor are they waiting for a man to begin their lives. Having made sacrifices for relationships in the past, they are less willing to give up what they have for a romantic relationship in which they feel they may be worse-off. Therefore, any male partner needs to amplify a woman's life and add value to it – and men are not used to this shift in the power dynamic. The women who do find romantic fulfilment later in life tend to do so with men who have done the emotional work and offer true partnership.

Women can no longer be scared into putting up with sub-par relationships, and this is HUGE, given the endless pressure most have received during the course of their lives – not just from men, by the way, but also from older women and female peers around needing to be in a relationship. *You're too fussy, you might die alone, you may never meet anyone else.* I wonder how many of us have stayed in damaging relationships because we were told to 'try and make things work', or because 'men are just being men'. For the first time in our lives we are learning to trust our own instincts because we know our feelings are valid.

* * *

When I was younger, dating was a means to an end – finding a boyfriend. The boyfriend would unlock everything – love, acceptance, happiness. However, my expectations of men, as someone growing up in the nineties, were lower than the limbo stick Shemika Campbell shimmied under for the Guinness World Record. (Twenty-two centimetres, if you are curious.) I expected very little of my dates, other than that they be interested in me. If they texted me, that was a sign they were a good person. See also: making me food, arranging a date, holding my hand in public.

Although my relationship with Rob ended up leading to so much pain, there were good parts, not least knowing and loving him. And, in return, being loved by him allowed me to love the parts of myself that I previously couldn't. When I went back to dating after his death, everything had changed. I knew what it was like to feel loved and be respected by someone, and I couldn't go back to that version of me that would make excuses and allow myself to be treated badly.

When I started dating again, I wasn't looking for love, or trying to replace that which was irreplaceable. I started because there was a part of myself that wanted to *feel*. That craved connection and sex. I wanted to lose myself in someone, to not have to think, to become undone, to dissolve. And I did, for a time.

For the latter half of my thirties, however, I felt as if my brain was being pulled apart. On the one hand, the traditional path of dating to find a partner didn't fit anymore. I wasn't dating to get into a relationship that would eventually lead to getting married. After Rob's death, people would ask about my love life with hope in their eyes, thinking I might meet someone and get married again and not be so sad, but I knew I didn't want that.

SHE WANTED MORE

I had never questioned my role as a married woman, but now that I had experienced it, I was far more wary. Not just because of the struggle around his health, but because I now understood the scale of what it means to have a partner, from shared finances to interminable conversations around housework, and the interrupted sleep that comes with sharing a bed.

A year after his passing, I'd set up the first home I'd ever lived in by myself, creating a peaceful, plant-filled haven. I wasn't all that keen to return to a relationship, and my body needed to feel again – more so than my mind. But I didn't feel it was permissible to voice my desires. It felt shameful, covert, base. Something that belonged to a different kind of person, certainly not a South Asian woman with stretch marks on her breasts.

Perhaps I would have gone on feeling this way, but then came the pandemic. And it changed everything when I went back onto dating apps, and in addition to the usual suspects such as Tinder and Hinge, I also tried non-traditional apps like Feeld.

Previously, I felt as if I needed to pretend to be a different person on dates. Someone who hid their desires and wants, because of how women must perform their femininity to be palatable to men. I didn't want a relationship, but I also wanted respect and connection with my lovers, and previously I was told that was impossible. 'Casual encounters mean you're going to be treated like shit,' a married friend told me, and I retorted with: 'Oh, and being in a relationship means you never are, I suppose?'

But my new experiences showed me that it was possible to have both. During my years using Feeld, I met some incredible people, had some of the most honest and respectful conversations about desire, in a way I never had on other apps. While I wouldn't say it is for everybody, it changed what I thought were the options. And it also made me realise that you should never, ever accept being treated like shit in any scenario.

So much of dating as a younger person is about numbing your own instincts; and what I have learned as a middle-aged woman is that how someone makes you *feel* about yourself is the most important thing. I don't mean the gifts they buy you, or the romantic gestures they make – that stuff really doesn't matter, even if it is your love language. I mean: do they amplify what is already there? Does this person light you up? Do they make you feel peaceful? Do they make you feel safe? And if your instinctive answer is no, then you don't need to analyse whether they are into you or respect you – they don't.

This person isn't a villain; they just aren't the right person for you. And knowing that, as you get older, and being able to walk away from it with kindness for yourself, and them, is power.

* * *

Having witnessed other people's unhappy marriages or having experienced them ourselves, we know the right person is worth waiting for. We also know that we cannot spend another minute centring our lives around the pursuit of a soulmate. I always laugh when a married friend responds to a bad dating story of mine: 'Thank God I'm not on the dating circuit', as if their coupled existence is preferable. I often want to reply: 'If I had to deal with your partner every day, I'd run over my own feet with a lawnmower', but I fear that would be a way to lose friends.

From what other women tell me, as well as my own experience, dating in your forties and beyond is no harder or easier than in other decades. It might *feel* harder because your standards have improved, and the offering hasn't. Present-day me would NEVER go on a date with someone just because they asked, if I knew I wasn't attracted to their personality. Twenty-something me would have.

It may be harder to find a long-term partner because the majority of people in their forties and fifties are married, and because you might be more particular than you were in your younger years. But that's not a bad thing. If you don't want to share your bed because you don't want terrible sleep, that is completely understandable. If you need the other person to demonstrate some understanding of equal rights, you're not being picky. If communicating about money is important to you and the other person doesn't want to discuss it, it's okay to say 'see you later'.

Finding your own people to talk to about this is essential. Your married friends can be warm and supportive but they are not the people you really need. Friends in long-term marriages, in particular, have no frame of reference around dating apps. They will probably suggest meeting someone 'in real life' instead because when they were last single, that's how it was done. It's convenient revisionist history, forgetting the many nights spent trawling clubs looking to meet someone special, and instead going home with a lukewarm kebab.

It also doesn't have to be one or the other. You can use dating apps, *and* meet someone organically – the point here is to keep yourself open to connection, and have high enough standards to ensure that you only date people you like.

I was reminded of the power of intention when I talked to Juno Dawson, one of my favourite authors and trans activists, about the biggest decisions in her life. She said that the decision to transition was undoubtedly the biggest, but one of the others was to make the choice in her late thirties to date for love. 'That changed the course of my life,' she said. 'I was in a bad routine of having flings and so I knew what I needed in a partner and it wasn't someone who was good in bed. It was someone who was kind, funny and compassionate. And that changed how I dated.' When she turned forty, she and her husband Max Gallant got married, in the South Downs.

It is a reminder to go into dating remembering who you are, and all that you are, rather than looking to someone else for the answer. They will only ever be able to show you a pale reflection at best, when in fact you comprise an entire universe.

* * *

It's important to talk about desirability, because something I have often heard from women my age or older is: 'who would be interested in me?' And they say that because of the lie that we've been fed, which is that we become less desirable, and less attractive, the older we get. One of the most desirable things you can do is to spend time with yourself and treat yourself as you would a romantic partner. (And I think this applies to everyone, whether you are single or not.)

'I've never questioned taking myself out on dates,' said Shannon. 'I'm not going to miss out on all the world has to offer because I don't have a romantic partner to accompany me. And you never know what might happen. I was on a solo holiday in Mallorca last year and was upgraded to a fabulous room for the week. I was feeling good after a few days in the sun and decided I wanted a holiday romance.

'Cue some swiping on Feeld and I connected with a great man, older than anyone I'd previously dated but charming, funny and very attractive, a few days of texting and we went for lunch. We talked and flirted non-stop and then went back to my room for a most wonderful sexual encounter. It was only ever going to be what it was, a beautiful moment in time, mutually respectful with no expectations on either of us other than having a lot of fun together.'

One of the most surprising revelations in my forties was how many younger men wanted to date me, and this is a story I hear over and over from other women in the dating pool. Having dated a wide spectrum of men, including those around ten years younger than me, younger men seem marginally more evolved around their feelings, gender equality and political issues than Gen X and elder millennial men.

While there's a danger in forming your sense of self around the desires of men, the interest of younger men overturns the idea that your attractiveness diminishes as you get older, or indeed, that attractiveness is purely aesthetic. 'I do think men respond positively not only to our general confidence in our forties,' Shannon said, 'but also regarding setting boundaries, and I wish I'd realised this sooner. I've definitely noticed an increase in younger guys approaching me, which is entertaining. It's nice to feel sexually desired especially as an older woman with a physical disability, a demographic largely deemed asexual.'

Men my age often find it hard to believe that I have options or that men younger than them would be interested in me, because they've been taught that women over a certain age are not desirable. I can't shake the feeling that they think I should be grateful for the attention, when the reality is that dating has never been as diverse or filled with options for me. I don't really date people much younger than me as a rule because I don't find youthfulness or inexperience attractive, but it's flattering to have the choice.

I talked to my friend Helen Thorn, a comedian, author and podcaster, about dating. Helen first came to my attention when she came out of a terrible situation with her ex-husband, who cheated on her. She wrote about it in her book *Get Divorced, Be Happy*, after finding herself back on the dating scene with two kids in tow, aged forty-one. (She is now forty-seven and in a happy relationship.)

When we first met, she was one of the few women talking openly about dating and sex in her forties, which was refreshing because I felt that a lot of my peers were in long-term relationships where sex wasn't a massive feature. And I was still being held back by a sense of shame around sex, which stemmed from my own culture as well as the general taboo that surrounds it.

'When I was in the throes of dating lots of different men of all ages,' she said, 'I was initially confused why I got so many matches with younger men. I was completely flattered they wanted an older lover, but maybe they made a mistake – surely they wanted some tiny younger lady?

'Quite the contrary. Many times I was told by younger men that they preferred older women, because of our confidence and knowing what we wanted. It was almost like both younger men and older women weren't looking for anything other than pleasure and fun and that there was a match in desire and energy.'

Like Helen, I've spent the last few years dating people of all ages, and it has taught me so much about myself – not just what I perceive to be red flags, but also green flags. Although there is currently a valid outpouring from women who have been disappointed when dating men – as we saw in the reaction to Lily Allen's *West End Girl* album and Chanté Joseph's *Vogue* article mentioned earlier – I don't think languishing in pessimism is of any practical benefit to women who do want meaningful romantic connection, not to mention physical touch.

The hugely popular TV show *Nobody Wants This*, with Kristen Bell, was such a perfect example of green flag behaviour while dating. In it, she meets Adam Brody's character Noah, and at every step she waits for him to ghost her or get freaked out. (Spoiler – he doesn't.) We all fell in love with Noah precisely because he represented what so many of us want in a man but feel it's impossible to find – someone who communicates with you, shows you he likes you and makes you feel safe.

In an interview with the *Wall Street Journal*, CEO and businesswoman Mellody Hobson, who is married to director George Lucas, said that his green flag when they first met was his reaction when she said she was worried she was calling him too much. 'He said you can call me anytime you want to call me. And I knew there was nothing I had to consider . . . was I overdoing or underdoing it? I knew he was the one when I knew there were no games.'

My green flags – regardless of gender – is how the person treats other people, especially people who work in the service industry. Whether they remember important events I've told them about – especially work milestones – and how they support and celebrate me. A major green flag is someone respecting my time, and making sure to check in and communicate if they are busy and can't be in touch as much as they'd like. I love reciprocity, and while I don't expect the other person to like the same things I do, I need to know they can organise and plan things for both of us. That it's not just me doing the work. If they are interested in my life, then I know they are interested in me as a person – not just in what I can give them. And people talk trash about dating, but I wouldn't have known anything about my green flags if I'd just been sitting at home refusing to engage.

Regardless of where you are in your journey – an observer from the stands of a relationship, someone on the fence of singledom or someone new to it – there is a lot to learn from women who date in the second and third act, in terms of how high they set the bar, and the beautiful things they fill their lives with. It's about operating from a place of fullness rather than scarcity, of neutrality rather than pessimism. It may sound like semantics but, when it's done right, the entire world opens at your feet, full of intention and possibility. And while dating can sometimes be dispiriting, no bad date I've been on has ever been as bad as my worst relationship.

CHAPTER NINE

SEX AND SEXUALITY

When I think about my sex education, it was distilled into two short lessons. The first was my mother saying 'Don't disappoint us' when I went on my first trip away with school friends aged sixteen – greatly over-estimating my success with boys. And the second was a sex education 'special' in our biology class, which consisted of a substitute teacher handing us a quiz which had sperm with smiley faces dotted around the questions.

'What have they got to be so fucking happy about?' my classmate said, tapping at our worksheet with a ruler. 'No idea,' I said, shrugging. And I didn't. About happy sperm or about anything to do with sex, only that being at a girls' school meant we talked about it *all the time*. About who was still a virgin, who would lose their virginity to 'insert name of rock star here', and who had already lost their virginity. A major setback was when one of our teenage classmates fell pregnant, and just as Leah Betts' tragic death in 1995 put us off doing drugs, so too was this a cautionary tale about what sex could lead to. A baby and being stuck in Dartford – birthplace of smallpox and Mick Jagger – forever.

With such a tragic lack of sex education from school and our parents, most of us learned about it through trial and error. Either through having sex (and, if you're anything like me, with people who also didn't have a clue what they were doing), talking about it with friends (who also didn't have a clue what they were doing) or seeing it on TV and in films (with scripts that were mainly written by sweaty middle-aged men perving over young women). Not only did this lack of information lead to fairly mediocre sex, but I think it also contributed to a disconnection from our bodies around pleasure. This can get further compounded as we age and feel there is less opportunity to change things up.

'Women don't realise how much pleasure they sacrifice daily,' said Ashley Kelsch, who writes about sex as well as middle age. 'They are conditioned to be in service and pleasing mode, constantly scanning for other people's needs before their own. That doesn't just show up in the bedroom – it's baked into how we move through the world. Reclaiming our sexual agency in midlife isn't just about sex. It's about sovereignty.'

The 'She Wanted More' survey results were telling: 36% of all women said they were not happy with their sex lives; 36% said they were happy with them sometimes; 69% said they had never read a sex book or taken a course to improve their sex lives. A salient fact is that 67% of all women who took the survey are in relationships.

But it doesn't have to be this way, and for an increasing number of women in midlife and beyond, sex is evolving. In the last few years, we have seen a groundswell of women talking about sex. And not just white women, but women from all backgrounds, which is especially crucial for people (like me) who come from cultures that are more conservative around sex.

'A lot of women might be thinking that, okay, my life doesn't really end at a certain age,' said Dr Pragya Agarwal. 'That I am still a sexual being. I'm still sexually desirable. And if you are not getting fulfilment, then perhaps women are looking to live fully and be the whole person they are and not conform to the kind of heteronormative social ideas of what relationships and marriages ought to be and how women should live their life.'

This view is echoed by Dr Karen Gurney, who is one of the leading national experts on this topic, a consultant clinical psychologist and certified psychosexologist. 'Women have an increase in their sexual confidence the older they get,' she told me, 'and we know that women are able to throw off the shackles of the male gaze. So you get this uptick in sexuality, which is about confidence, rejecting beauty standards, and understanding their own capacity for pleasure and not wanting to settle for less than that. Now you have heterosexual women who are asking themselves, "why shouldn't I be experiencing pleasure?", in a way that in their twenties, they would have just accepted any sex as long as the man was happy.'

One of the women who changed my entire perspective around sex as we age is the sexual health influencer and author Seema Anand (who has over a million followers on Instagram). Seema is in her sixties, and aside from looking like a literal goddess with her flowing silver hair and red lipstick, is also an exquisite storyteller. She uses lessons from the Kama Sutra, the OG text about sex and desire, to illustrate and teach many lessons around arousal and sexual dynamics, as well as women taking delight in their own bodies.

One of the first things she told me was that the absence of what we've been taught is as significant as what we have actually been taught. For many of us, women's pleasure has almost always taken second place to men's, and it begins with the chastity myth.

'We don't tell stories of a woman's pleasure,' she said. 'We tell stories of a woman's body being property. And the most common story is the power of chastity. In every culture we have this thing called the chaste woman. If you are chaste, then you are "good" and then you have power. And there is a deifying of chastity to the point where we had women almost hustle to be on that pedestal.'

It made me think of how women's 'body counts' are discussed by podcast bros, and how a woman is deemed 'high value' if she hasn't slept with many men. Conversely, how 'chastity' is never a term applied to men. It made me think about how women are incentivised around their chastity – promises of status, a reputation of 'goodness' – and how their 'honour' is tied to it in a way that it isn't for men. Although I don't have brothers, I knew enough South Asians at university to know the double standards for boys were terrible – they were allowed to go out all hours, and sleep with whoever they wanted, while the girls were constantly policed.

There is also the double bind that when a man cheats, it is because men aren't 'designed to be monogamous due to primal urges' – which is a convenient bending of science. 'Social, economic and cultural factors all shape sexual behaviour,' my friend Dr Rishita Nandagiri told me. She works as a feminist researcher and lecturer at King's College London, and said that discussion of monogamy is also gendered and we have to consider the 'sexual stigma and shaming that ciswomen face and the massive gap in orgasms.' She added, 'Behaviourally, if heterosexual men are experiencing pleasurable sex where pleasure = orgasms, and heterosexual women are largely not... it also stands to reason that women may be more "picky" about when they engage.'

Evolutionary biologists find it hard to agree on these issues because it is difficult to separate social and biological factors. Human beings generally aren't sexually monogamous, but they have evolved to be *socially* monogamous because of things like child-rearing.

'There's a weird idea that we are solely there to propagate,' Seema said, 'and behind this is the subliminal narrative of the woman's pleasure not being particularly important. We never talk of a woman's pleasure. We never tell stories of how the woman lies back (sated) at the end of it. She's always satisfied with the love that she gets, the caring, or sacrifices she makes, but there are no stories told of satisfaction from being satisfied physically.'

We are lucky to live in a time of women empowering other women around sex, helping them to unlearn and remove shame, as well as expanding the depictions of older women in literature, TV and film. We are figuring out the messy parts of a woman's identity and sexual experience – with all the other layers, from how we feel hormonally to what we want to try sexually.

It cannot be called a reclamation, because women have never been empowered to centre their own sexual needs, and to truly own their desire. But it can be called a reckoning, and it isn't just for single women who have the freedom to explore, but for women who are in relationships who want and deserve more from their sex lives and should not be made to feel ashamed about it.

'When a woman writes to me,' Seema continued, 'a lot of the time, she'll say, "I want more sex, but each time I say it to my partner, he'll say *that's all you ever think about*". It's about undoing and interrupting that constant shaming.'

This seismic shift around sex isn't just about hetero women and their male partners. In some cases it has been women (including me) figuring out new aspects of their sexuality. Overall, it is about expanding the idea of what we know about sex. The pandemic saw a massive increase in people, especially heterosexuals, looking to experiment, sexually including things such as kink and non-monogamy, and practices that would frankly make your average vanilla friend blush. There has been a massive boom in sex parties since the pandemic, and although this has largely been driven by millennials, there are also people in their forties and fifties looking for a safe environment to push their boundaries that would be unacceptable in their everyday lives.[34]

Miranda July's novel *All Fours* was published in 2024, and since then it has been constantly referenced in any conversation around sex and women over forty. July has created a space on her Substack for women to have honest, gritty conversations around sex and sexual identity in a way I haven't seen many other authors doing. The 2024 film *Babygirl*, starring Nicole Kidman as a fifty-something CEO who embarks on a sexual kink-discovery journey with her young male intern, divided opinion. But even if you didn't like the narrative, it was undeniable that it reflected a shift around the agency and ownership of wanting and needing sex.

Tech CEO Cindy Gallop talks openly about sex in her sixties, and has created a platform called MakeLoveNotPorn, as an alternative to hardcore porn which she believes is warping people's expectations of sex. And Gillian Anderson's book *Want*, featuring anonymous stories about sexual fantasies, led to many conversations for older women around desire.

Former magazine editor and podcast host Lorraine Candy wrote in *The Guardian*, 'Our generation (Gen X) came of age with Samantha Jones's racy one-liners in *Sex and the City* and expert sex tips from the magazines we edited. We were vocal about our desires and libido and need for sex all through our 20s and 30s – so why would we not want that . . . [in] our sex lives as we age? Sex matters to us.'[35]

There are a vast number of newsletters about sex for women in midlife and beyond. One of my favourites is

To The Bed', penned by a woman using the pseudonym Loretta, who writes about her sexual adventures as a forty-something divorcee and mother.

'I am starting to change my beliefs and expectations about pleasure,' she told me, 'which makes me feel more comfortable with my body. For instance, for a long time, I worried that men didn't like performing oral sex on me – that I had too much hair, that I smelled, that my vulva was ugly. I think that belief was rooted in the idea that sex and pleasure exist primarily for men.

'Men's pleasure has long been centred, so whenever a man focused on my pleasure, I assumed it was performative – that he didn't really want to be doing it, that he was just going through the motions. It didn't help that, in my twenties, I often gave blowjobs out of a sense of duty and not because I wanted to or enjoyed them. Now I'm realising that men can and do enjoy giving women pleasure – and that I am worthy of receiving it. Interestingly, I now enjoy giving blowjobs a lot more, too.'

After the increased conversation around sex for midlife and older women, there have been grumblings online about how women now feel pressured to engage in wild, adventurous sex when they actually feel fed-up and tired. Personally, the perceived pressure feels like a projection – no one is forcing people to do anything they don't want to do, and talking about sex as we grow older is necessary. Women who suppress their own sexual desire and continue to have unfulfilling sex because they are told their pleasure isn't important, or because they are stuck in sexless relationships and are made to feel ashamed about their unhappiness about it, need some validation and a way through.

Cindy Gallop spoke to me from her New York apartment and expressed her strong feelings about this: 'Let's say you want to have sex, but your partner doesn't. There are a number of people who are okay with that and don't see that as a big enough reason to leave or have a conversation to do something about it. The acceptance around that, is something I find mind-blowing. I just think, okay, so you're in your forties, fifties, sixties whatever. You may live for another twenty, thirty, forty years, and you don't need to be resigned to [a life without sex].'

Ekin, who took the 'She Wanted More' survey, said she tried to have a conversation about the lack of sex she and her partner were having, but nothing changed. 'As we don't live together, the time we are together is limited to weekends and the odd week. There is constant miscommunication, and I grew tired of being rejected quickly and stopped instigating. For Valentine's Day he went down on me and I realised I don't want to feel like I'm begging or feel grateful when he touches me. I'm leaving him.'

While doing research for this book around sexless long-term relationships, I came across Hannah, fifty-nine, who is married with two adult children. Hannah messaged me to say that the conversations started by Miranda July on her Substack – which are framed in such a non-judgemental way – made her feel less alone and encouraged her to share her story.

Her marriage has been sexless for over twenty years, after her last child was born, which led to an absence of any kind of physical affection, even touch. When her children were younger and she was cuddling them and hugging them, she didn't notice the absence of touch as much, but when they both left home, it became an enormous issue.

'I also had a hysterectomy and started HRT,' she said. 'This combination of factors raised the question: "Are you prepared to die without ever having sex again?" The answer was no.' Hannah ended up sleeping with a man in his thirties, and after that went on apps to chat to different younger men. 'I felt so free to be a version of me that I hadn't seen for so long but with the added benefit of being older and wiser. I felt younger and hotter than ever before and it was wonderful.'

Hannah went on to meet up with more men, which made her feel in charge of her own sexual satisfaction. 'I had looked to my marriage to fulfil me,' she said, 'and when it didn't, I was angry. My husband seems quite relieved that I have stopped giving him a hard time. He does sometimes raise an eyebrow about me doing things alone like going to gigs in London, but he spends so much time on golf and sport trips with other men so he doesn't have a leg to stand on. So many of the men in my social circle lack energy and drive and passion. I don't think my husband would ever understand why a young guy would want to be with me.'

Hannah's husband doesn't know about her affairs, but because they offer the intimacy she needs, I imagine she reconciles any guilt with being able to exist within the marriage as a result.

'My friends (who are married) know my story,' she said.

SHE WANTED MORE

'But I think they have got to the point now where they would rather not hear every second of what I am up to.'

Hearing Hannah's story forced me to confront the feelings that came up. On the one hand, I feel sorry for her husband who doesn't know about the infidelity, and on the other hand, I feel as if I am witnessing someone trying to survive their life and keep everyone happy. When I see these kinds of stories in agony aunt columns, and read the angry comments aimed at the person cheating, it's clear that it is viewed in a binary way, but I'm not sure it is that simple.

In a 2017 interview with *The Guardian*, when her controversial book *The State of Affairs: Rethinking Infidelity* came out, Esther Perel touched on this. 'I don't think it can be reduced to good and bad, victim and perpetrator,' she said to journalist Lucy Rock. 'We need a conversation that embraces the complexity and that is more caring and compassionate for everybody involved. So yes, an affair always involves a breach of trust and it's an act of betrayal. It involves lies, secrecy. But there are all kinds of things happening in the relationship, and betrayal sometimes comes in many forms.'[36]

After reading Hannah's story, I went for a long walk in the warm summer evening to see what thoughts arose in the quiet. Surrounded by fields of amber, I'd subconsciously chosen a route I used to take a lot during the pandemic, that I now visited infrequently. Although there was a lot about that time I'd tried to forget, from social distancing to toilet paper shortages, one memory pushed to the fore – what it was like not to have any physical touch for months. Even now, my body recoils and wants to think of something, anything else. Physical contact is a physiological need, and therefore, the lack of it – which is sometimes referred to as skin hunger or touch starvation – can be very harmful to our sense of confidence and ability to regulate our emotions.

Although we might feel judgemental about people who have made the kinds of decisions Hannah has made, we don't truly know how we might feel if someone we have built an entire life with decides to withhold something so fundamental to being human.

* * *

If you are stuck in a sexless situation with your long-term partner who you love very much and have no wish to leave or be unfaithful to, there are options.

'People think that not having sex for a while is uncommon,' Dr Gurney told me. 'But it's much more common than you'd think. Most people, she said, over-estimate how much they should be having and then feel bad about not having enough. 'The average tends to be about twice a month, if that.'

Your sex life may drop off for a number of reasons. 'Desire is quite hard to maintain in long-term relationships without intentional effort,' she said. 'It's not impossible, but most people don't realise they have to do it. What tends to happen is that people think, if you love the person, then you should feel the desire to have sex with them, and that should come out of the blue. And we call that spontaneous desire. You get a lot of that at the start of a relationship, and then around about eighteen months in, give or take, it tends to tail off as we see upticks in familiarity, and as we see other dynamics change in the relationship.

'Dynamics like living together, having kids, but also just the predictability and familiarity of a partner reduce our levels of spontaneous desire. Sexual satisfaction is at its lowest when you've got a kid under five in the house. It's partly connected to sleep, partly connected to life admin, and the mental load comes in there, because for heterosexual women, particularly, they're carrying the burden of that. And I think for women in this age group, this is a really big factor.'

Dr Gurney refers to 'sexual currency', which is dependent on how good your communication is with each other, and how connected you feel. Unsurprisingly, when women feel as if they have to take care of their partners and treat them like children that greatly reduces their sex drive. So this currency declines the longer you go without having sex, because then doubt creeps in around who initiates what and when.

A problem that seems to crop up time and again is the scenario in which a woman tries to talk to her partner about their sex life, but they don't want to talk about it. And it's more likely to happen with men, who are more emotionally shut down in comparison.

Dr Gurney's advice is simple and to the point. 'It's common for people to struggle to talk about sex, so don't be too disheartened if someone seems reluctant or they don't engage with it at first. I'd advise talking about the meaning of sex for you and for the relationship, not just the act of sex itself. So, for example, you might say: "I really miss the way our sex life used to be. And I loved how when we were having sex, we used to feel more close and more connected. I would really like to get back to that, because I worry that if we don't, we might drift apart emotionally." That's a very different way of explaining it, compared to "we never have sex anymore, and what are you going to do about it?"'

I asked women who follow me on Instagram, who were forty-plus and in long-term relationships, for advice on how they reset a long period of no sex. The answers were surprisingly heartwarming.

'The side-effects of my cancer treatment,' wrote Megan, 'meant sex was on the back burner for a long time (and still not back to where it was before). We've not had spontaneous, P in V sex for about three years now, however we've continued being as intimate as we can throughout that time. It's been an emotional and physical shitshow – but one thing it has done is help me truly understand just how much my husband loves and cares for me, the depth of his patience and understanding, and also how sex (although lovely) is not the be-all and end-all of a happy relationship. All of this combined means that there is now far less pressure, we communicate much better, and we appreciate the smaller acts of intimacy/celebrate the wins more!'

'We stopped having sex when I was nursing my dying mum,' Aleesha wrote in. 'I was staying with her and when it was finally over we moved house and somehow stopped having sex. Two years went by, neither of us spoke about it. It became a huge issue for me. We did eventually have "the conversation" and we went away for a few days later that month and re-started having sex. Strangely we found it helpful to read all the emails we sent each other when we were first together and having sex at every opportunity.'

'During lockdown we actually had a "sex weekend",' said Aarti, 'where I just bought loads of stuff (underwear/toys) from Ann Summers and we just used that to kickstart our sex life again. We also communicate regularly. I have a much higher sex drive than him – the myth that men are always up for it and women aren't is SUCH bullshit! What works for us is actually scheduling. It doesn't sound sexy but we have completely different body clocks. He's a zombie in the morning and I am super grumpy if I'm not in bed by 10. Sunday afternoon is usually our go-to. The main change in our preferences is using toys – it should be taught during sex ed. We had good sex before but by using vibrators etc. it's now so much better for me.'

'Menopause stripped me of my libido and sex became a chore,' Agnes said. 'I didn't feel any sexual urge. Started HRT and it took a few months but suddenly it returned with a vengeance and for the last year I've had the libido of a teen boy!'

* * *

My views and understanding of sex are markedly different to how they were in my twenties and thirties. Until I met Rob, I hadn't ever met a man who understood how to centre a woman's pleasure. I was always led by them. I didn't understand anything about my own body, what I could ask for, how I wanted to feel, and what pleasure and desire looked like for me. Thinking about that time is like looking at a black-and-white photo. I was there, but it was empty of true enjoyment and reciprocity.

Rob was shocked when I told him that he was the first man who'd ever made me feel truly desired, and he was angry when I told him about the men who'd made me feel as if my body was disgusting. With him, I felt worshipped and adored.

When I stepped back into dating after he passed away, the imperative wasn't to find a connection or a relationship. That part of myself was still lost in grief, still in love with Rob, still unable to give anything much to anyone. But those first flickers of life showed up in my body. They held the first seedling of hope, the core primal urge to survive, to feel.

Unlike all the other times I dated, I was very clear about what I wanted. Yes I wanted to go on dates, yes I wanted sex, but I didn't want anything more than that. Perhaps it was a ribbon of good karma coming back to help me, but the first person I dated ended up being the perfect person I needed for that point in time. I'll call him Eric. He worked in tech, and was pretty much a lifelong bachelor who had no intention of changing his lifestyle. That suited me just fine, especially because he held a balance between kindness and tentative naughtiness.

The first time he came back to my place, I freaked out about the idea of someone seeing my body naked. It had been *so long* and I had no sense of love for my body. It had nothing to do with body size and everything to do with *what will he think? Will he find me disgusting? What about this patch of pigmentation?* And for anyone going through the same thing,

SHE WANTED MORE

it's hard to know where to start, especially if you haven't had sex for a while, or you're navigating sex as a midlife woman with new lovers.

'Being naked is a vulnerable thing, I know, but also incredibly freeing,' said Helen Thorn, when I asked her about the first time she started to have sex as a newly single person. 'I have had two children, so there's stretch marks, wrinkles, and of course random hairs aplenty, but that didn't seem to matter in the throes of passion. And always, after a couple of wines, some flattering low lighting, and some helpful lingerie, I felt pretty damn fabulous. I never once heard a man apologise for his body, so I just decided to be free of that shame thrown on us women.'

For women who come from more sexually conservative cultures, it can be hard to feel a connection with our naked bodies because so much of what we've been made to feel is shame. Not just because we've been told that our bodies should be covered up, but because as a brown teenager, and then as a young woman, I didn't see women who looked like me, who *were* me, playing those roles. We were not the romantic lead, ever, unless it was a film directed by a South Asian person.

My entire mood board was all the women in Mira Nair's film *Kama Sutra* – oiled brown skin, pearls, jasmine, ornate hair, breasts undulating like the surface of the sea, and when I finally met Indira Varma (who played the main character) in person, I regret to say I was an intense little weirdo. But what I told her was true. I saw what desire could look like, and it was painted in the colour of my skin. When I did finally let Eric in, I anchored myself to that sense of belonging and beauty, and found that my body was something to luxuriate in. It had curves, it was beautiful, it had survived so much. And that love, that sense of connection with my own body, radiated out.

A few years later, I read an interview in *The Cut* with one of my favourite authors, Mira Jacob, whose comments about her body resonated so strongly, I hold on to them whenever I show a new lover my body. 'Every time I've slept with somebody,' she said, 'they've been so psyched about the juiciness of my body, but that's not really a message you see out in the world. The biggest evolution for me was the understanding that my body's known truths have always been valid.'[37]

Like a lot of women, I'd been made to feel so grateful for even a speck of positivity about my body for most of my life. What I realised is that most people – whatever their gender – are usually so happy to be there with you, with the prospect of whatever your joint desire creates, they are not bothering with the million things you're worried about when it comes to your own body.

'There are a number of women who write in and say they have pigmentation on their upper thighs or labia,' Seema said, 'and ask how they can get a vagina whitening cream. I have never come across a man saying "I need a penis whitening cream." A guy doesn't even consider that when he is having sex with his partner, that she will be looking at his balls not being the same colour as his penis. All testicles have pigmentation.

'He would not even consider you would look or comment on it, or that it would detract in any way from the pleasure you are likely to feel. Yet for women, there is this whole thing that you are not perfect enough and hence don't have the right to pleasure.'

How you feel about your body matters more than you think. A 2019 study of sexually active women with a mean age of fifty-eight showed that 'women who felt self-conscious about their bodies reported that these concerns had a negative impact on their sexual satisfaction, whereas women who felt confident discussed better sexual satisfaction, even in the face of bodily changes.' Black women in this age demographic were more likely to discuss feeling confident than white women.[38]

Your body is never going to be perfect, and its reflection will always shift depending on who is holding a mirror up to it. But we can change how we feel about it in a way that isn't dependent on outside validation. One of those tools is doing a workshop. People tend to think of sex workshops as ones that deal with technique but, increasingly, there are a number that help us to focus on ourselves first, and to dismantle deeply rooted shame.

Henika Patel – a British South Asian practitioner whose dad was an ex-monk turned artist – runs the School of Sensual Arts. 'In a world where images of the perfect body are everywhere,' she told me, 'many of us find an impossible standard to achieve as we turn off the lights and take off our clothes. We correlate our stretch marks, wrinkles and curves to our self-worth and our love-making ability to our body image. But real connection and intimacy goes beyond shape, looks and size. My work uses the tools of Tantra, yoga and Ayurveda (the Indian sister sciences) with a blend of western therapeutic models.'

One of her practices includes an exercise called 'nyasa', which is literally simply touching each part of the body and infusing it with positive affirmations. 'You can do this while you moisturise every day or in the shower as you soap,' she said. "These are my powerful legs", "this is my beautiful face" etc. Any time your mind wanders, bring your attention back to where you feel the touch. This practice will create a new script and translate into the bedroom or you can even ask a partner to do it with you in foreplay.'

This infusion of love and worth into our bodies is important because in the survey, nearly 40% of women over forty said they had trouble feeling as if they were desirable. These feelings are not insignificant, especially when we are actively disempowered around sex in our forties and beyond – whether that's how we are depicted (or not), how we are included (or not) or having spent a lifetime believing that men's pleasure matters more than our own.

* * *

Talking about sex is important because of the frightening reputation peri-menopause and menopause have, concerning our libidos. I've been told a number of times menopause kills libido but our experiences of menopause can vary a lot, and libido is not just based on our hormones but can also be impacted by environment and stress.

Regarding the menopause, some experience a loss of libido, while others may feel it's the same. Some experience no physical symptoms that impact sex, while others experience symptoms due to the drop in oestrogen that make sex extremely uncomfortable, such as vaginal dryness and Genitourinary Syndrome of Menopause (GSM) previously known as vaginal atrophy. GSM – the inflammation and thinning of the vagina that is related to the menopause – is still one of those topics that is only now emerging from taboo – 40 to 54% of women may experience it during the menopause, according to the National Institutes for Health,[39] and it increases in post-menopause to up to 80%.[40] But because so little is known about the condition, few seek help.

The TV show *Grace and Frankie* addressed this – Frankie talks about her homemade yam lube for post-menopausal women. There's actually a real-life duo who did this back in 2006 – former management consultants Susi Lennox and Sarah Brooks created an organic lubricant called YES. Initially, they made it with the needs of cancer patients in mind, who tended to lose moisture in their vaginas after treatment. They then found it to be a hit with menopausal women.

Even taking control of a particular aspect of your sex life, such as lubricant, is something new. Seema told me that in some relationships, men are reluctant to use lube because it's a point of pride. 'That's one of the most detrimental things I've come across,' she said. 'I get a lot of men in the comments section saying, *if you're a real man, she doesn't need lube.* There is this thing about her pleasure being secondary to your concept of your ego or masculinity.'

The great news is that because more women are now vocal about menopause and post-menopause, we are hearing much more varied stories about what it is like for them, when it comes to sex. And increasingly, I hear of women's libidos improving after menopause. When someone asked on Reddit, 'did menopause make your desire go away after it was over?', I rolled around on the floor laughing at one person's response: 'So far it's not slowing me down. Sometimes I wish it would.'

The post-menopausal community is such a vital part of visualising what lies beyond, especially when it comes to sex. Talking to our peers helps us navigate the storm, but I also need to hear from women in their sixties who are on the other side of things. One person who is visible and open about their sex life, as well as educating people in a similar situation, is Suzanne Noble, who started a podcast and social platform called *Sex Advice for Seniors*. She is in her mid-sixties.

'Your sex life is only over if you choose it to be,' she said to me. 'One of the great advantages of being older is the freedom to design your relationships without the burden of societal expectations. Take your time to consider what your ideal relationship would look like if no one were dictating what they thought it should look like.

'Maybe you're looking for intimacy without commitment, perhaps you want to connect with someone much younger, or maybe you prefer occasional encounters. There are so many ways to approach relationships later in life, including exploring same-sex relationships if that's a desire you've never realised.'

When I see Suzanne's unbelievably frank posts, from nudism to her ongoing situationship, I laugh, I cry, and mostly

SHE WANTED MORE

I am thankful for her work in this space, because she routinely breaks down the stereotypes I've built up in my own head around sex and desire for older people.

I wanted to ask her a bit more about her journey to this place of sexual liberation. 'I've been sexually active for most of my life,' she said, 'except for my marriage, during which I was celibate for the last four years. In my twenties, I was promiscuous, having sex with both men and women, though it all feels quite vanilla in retrospect. After my marriage ended in my forties, I embarked on a sexual journey of discovery, determined to fulfill every fantasy I had. I explored various alternative lifestyles – swinging, BDSM, tantra.'

When she turned fifty, Suzanne settled down monogamously with a man sixteen years her junior, but menopause was rough and a major contributor to their breakup, although they are now best friends. 'My libido took a nosedive, hot flashes became incredibly unpleasant, and I spent several years reconsidering how to experience sex and desire as an older woman,' she said.

In her late fifties, she got into another relationship, but after four years realised that a traditional, monogamous relationship wasn't making her happy. She went to Gran Canaria in 2021, decided to dip a toe back into the swinging world and found she still really enjoyed it. In the last year, she's been in a situationship and says it's stress-free, drama-free and the sex is great.

'I've become much more intentional about my sex life,' she added. 'I genuinely enjoy sex and the pleasure it brings, but feeling sexual now involves preparation, much like any other event. There's a ritual to it: showering, shaving, and wearing something that makes me feel sexy, along with soft music and candles. When my partner visits, we both invest significant energy into mutually satisfying each other in ways I probably wouldn't if we lived together.'

Regarding the trope that women are less interested in sex than men, she said: 'There's a prevailing assumption that older people, particularly women, don't engage in sexual activity. While some of my female friends fit this description, it's not entirely accurate. The lack of education on overcoming physical challenges – like unreliable erections in men and GSM in women – does little to dispel these stereotypes.'

When you consider that there is a little blue pill readily available to deal with male erectile problems, but there isn't when it comes to something like GSM (the inflammation and thinning of the vagina that can happen during menopause), it's hard not to get angry about the amount of extra work women still have to do around their health. 'Healthcare professionals are often poorly equipped to discuss sex and intimacy with older patients,' she said, 'and some of the accounts I've heard from my audience about their doctors' responses are horrifying. There's so much misinformation out there, it's no wonder people are confused and frustrated.'

So, when it comes to women and our pleasure, there are significant blockers that we are told stem from our lesser desire to have sex, but actually it is more complicated than that. It's not just physical changes, but also mental changes that occur. 'Arousal patterns in women change over time,' Suzanne said. 'If you expect to be turned on simply by looking at someone, that's unlikely. Arousal often shifts from being spontaneous to responsive. For me, this means I need physical touch – a kiss, a caress – to feel turned on. I have to trust my body will respond, rather than instinctively knowing it will.'

As women's pleasure hasn't been centred in the past, accessing this kind of knowledge and power about ourselves isn't easy. We aren't going to stumble across it; we have to seek it out. When you do, the next challenge is being able to communicate with your partner about what you want from sex, and if it is someone you have been with for decades, this can often feel tough.

If your partner is male, some can take it as an affront, which I believe is actually shame and embarrassment because they are told that their sexual prowess is so heavily woven into their masculinity. I've had lovers who have asked me to tell them what I want, and how I want it, and when it hasn't immediately worked, I then find myself caretaking their disappointment in themselves. Talk about a lady boner killer.

It is always a reminder, however, that none of us has anything to gain from our mindsets being so fixed. That shame has no place in our lives ever, but especially not as we grow older.

* * *

Sex and sexuality are two different topics, but I need to address one of the most significant differences in this current generation of midlife women, compared to previous generations, which is the increase in sexual fluidity. In other words, there are women who are realising their queer identity at a relatively late stage in life. (My advice to anyone who fits this description is to find queer women and non-binary friends as quickly as you can. Your hetero pals and cis-gender gay male friends may mean well, but they might not be that much help as you figure this out.)

Apart from a 2023 study, which noted the rise in women questioning societal expectations as they related to sex and sexuality, there isn't a huge amount of data on how this affects women over forty. That behavioural shift around sexuality seems a lot more prevalent across Gen Z and younger millennial women, who feel less need to define themselves rigidly.[41]

I realised I was probably pansexual at the grand age of forty and my first question was: *how did you not realise it before?* Mainly because it didn't feel like I'd repressed something or had been living a lie. It was more like finding an extra compartment that I didn't know was there. Once the truth emerged, I read a lot, watched a ton of TikToks, and realised that hetero-conformity is so intense that for some women, it remains hidden, like a seedling, until the right set of circumstances allow it to bloom.

At the beginning, I struggled with not knowing who I was, and then realised it wasn't really anyone's business. Mostly it meant unravelling the internalised homophobia I was surrounded by when I was growing up, including Section 28, which was in force when I was at school. (This 1988 law banned any discussion of LGBTQ+ in schools, which created an atmosphere of fear and implanted deep-rooted prejudices that homosexuality was something wrong or perverse.)

SHE WANTED MORE

Realising this in my forties has been a blessing in disguise – I see it as something good, something that allows me to live in technicolour. I've had to be intentional in finding out more about it in order to understand who I am; and the closest approximation I can find is that the older I get, the more I push against labels, and definitions. I am not wholly one thing, and the freedom I feel within that has been life-altering in every way. It has also forced me to seek community in different spaces, and it has led to me finding a queer friendship group who fill my life with light in a way I thought wasn't possible.

One of the people whose words resonated most strongly with me around this was the author and journalist Catherine Gray, who wrote the bestselling book *The Unexpected Joy of Being Sober*. I adore Catherine, who has been a supporter of my work, and when I saw her post on Instagram about figuring out that she was bisexual in her forties, I messaged her immediately. How did she feel about this realisation arriving so late?

'Reaching this in midlife meant it felt robust and unapologetic, a truth built on solid ground,' she said. 'Had I realised in my twenties, I would have been shaky, moveable, and asking for permission from everyone I told. Wondering what they said behind my back about it. Wondering if my female friends now thought I snuck glances at them in changing rooms. As a midlifer, I don't give a fig what anyone thinks about it or says about it. That's bloody lovely.'

Catherine only properly realised it when she was forty-three, and described it as being 'beautiful but jarring'. I strongly related. 'I think I packed myself into a box of compulsory heterosexuality early on,' she said, 'maybe as early as 11, when I experienced my first kiss at a sleepover with my best friend back then. After our "snogging practice", we curled up together like kittens.

'I don't recall feeling ashamed of it, and yet, on an innate level I believed I wasn't allowed to say my first kiss was with her. It didn't count, in my tween brain. I considered myself unkissed, until a boy came to kiss me. I would wrongly attribute my first kiss to him for the next 32 years.'

At university, she had a six-month relationship with a woman we'll call Sophie, but always thought of it as an experiment. She went on to date men, and then the realisation hit when she wrote a bisexual protagonist in her first novel, *Versions of a Girl*. 'Her relationship feels so real', a friend said to her, and Catherine realised that was because it was drawn from her own sexual identity. 'I started telling people, but was careful about who I told in person,' she said. 'I didn't feel any obligation to "come out" and many of my friends and family would have found out via the articles I then wrote about it. I don't owe them an explanation of my sexuality, any more than they owe me one about theirs.' I felt exactly the same about myself.

When I asked her if she wished she'd known earlier, she said: 'It arrives when it arrives. You can't accelerate, or force self-knowledge into landing early.'

Speaking to a wide range of women over the last few years, I've come to realise that there is no such thing as 'too late'. I don't know if we are more sexually fluid than we were before, but it is easier to accept and own the changes in our sexuality, and in some cases be more visible.

Even though the LGBTQ+ community is experiencing a hard time at the moment, due to legislative changes in places such as the US, and the suppression of its visibility in the mainstream, it is easier than it was when I was growing up. When I was younger, the South Asian LGBTQ+ community was non-existent, and now it flourishes in ways more beautiful than I could ever have hoped or imagined. In some ways, I feel I owe a lot to Gen Z, who don't accept or allow judgement around who they are.

It all comes down to the same thing, does it not? Wanting to be loved for everything that you are.

CHAPTER TEN

INTRODUCING THE CLIMACTERIC! (AKA ALL THINGS MENOPAUSAL)

When I was in my mid-thirties, I got a surprise gift from a major UK wellness supermarket. A menopause kit!

'What the fuck?' I said as I opened the box and found a white shapeless nightie that would have been fashionable before the invention of electricity. I dug further and found bottles of different vitamins. The message I took away was this: women in the menopause are ghosts who need pills to bolster their desiccating bones.

Even though it was ten years ago, the conversation around menopause was very different from what it is now. I remember the mix of my emotions: the anger that I was *far too young* for this, the fear at being reminded that menopause was in my future at some point, and the associations I had with that – loss of control, hysterics, dusty vagina, sweating, unhappiness. Menopause sounded life-ending.

I recently found out that the word used to describe the transition from a reproductive life to a non-reproductive life is *not* the menopause. The word menopause refers to a specific event – for instance, when your periods cease. But the entirety of it, from peri-menopause to menopause to post-menopause, is called the climacteric.

I love it as a word. Not just because menopause has such loaded, negative connotations, but because climacteric feels all-encompassing. And it sounds badass. Not an apocalypse which gives Bad Vibes, more like a cataclysm. Something enormous and life-altering, with a light sprinkling of death and destruction, with the capacity to create the kind of vibrant life afterwards that wasn't possible before.

The climacteric refers to the period when our oestrogen levels start to dip. Oestrogen controls our reproductive system, and when this hormone starts to drop it can cause fluctuations in our reproductive cycles, which show up as peri-menopause. Peri-menopause is meant to start in your mid-forties, but for some it can even begin as early as your late thirties.

This hormonal shift can prompt a whole range of symptoms, from night sweats to thinking everyone everywhere is a fucking idiot, no exceptions; then it transitions to menopause around the age of fifty, which is the time when a woman goes a full year without a period. After menopause, we enter a state called post-menopause, which is still a time in which we may have low hormone levels that need adjusting.

When I thought about what to include in this chapter, it felt impossible to include everything. Then I realised I didn't need to. We are lucky to live in a time where there are TV shows, books, podcasts and influencers who talk about this extensively. Sam Baker was one of the first, as were Mariella Frostrup and Davina McCall. The scope of this chapter, therefore, is to chart my own resistance around accepting the climacteric, and what I've learnt that might be helpful to others, as well as including the powerful and more positive aspects of menopause and post-menopause.

* * *

A big part of being in my forties has meant confronting what I think I know about menopause, overcoming my fears and finding the right people to talk to about it. Even though I'm only at the midpoint of the decade, a lot has happened since then that has been critical to understanding not just things about my own body, but how it affects the women around me and, on a macrocosmic level, failings around women's health.

When I entered my forties, I felt overloaded by the amount of discussion about peri-menopause. It manifested in two ways – either people spoke often and exclusively about their own symptoms; or they would convince me that I was in peri-menopause, and was I sure that I wasn't? Sometimes it made me question my own mind and it seemed *terrifying*. I didn't want to engage with it. Every time someone tried to talk to me about it, a wall quickly came up.

When I spoke to older women about this, however, they'd refer to the bad old days, when it wasn't spoken about at all – and they said that was far worse than the overload of information we're experiencing nowadays. This forced me to confront a few things.

The first was how women over fifty have historically been represented in the context of menopause on TV. The sweating was often used as a comedic device, and they were portrayed as hysterical and not to be trusted, because they were too governed by their hormones. The second was the lack of information about it, which meant that women were experiencing symptoms but thinking they were the only ones going through it. Not only must that have been isolating, but it also ended up having an enormously detrimental effect on some women who were experiencing symptoms such as brain fog and thinking it was early onset dementia.

A few years ago, I interviewed a police officer who took early retirement because she thought her cognitive function was severely impaired, when it was just the menopause. The lack of insight and education around menopause in the workplace also has a huge impact, because it can affect a woman's decision to stay in her job, due to her symptoms and loss of confidence in herself.

The third was how poorly equipped the healthcare system was, judging by the accounts of women who struggled to get the right kind of care, in terms of dealing with peri-menopause and menopause. The fourth is the lack of research on this stage of life. Given that women make up around 50% of the population and menopause is an inevitability, this lack of data is unacceptable.

When I chatted to the journalist and broadcaster Mariella Frostrup, who is the Chair of Menopause Mandate in the UK and US, about how to navigate the slew of information out there, she said: 'I think the societal expectation of women was to endure, and that to endure no matter what, whether it's childbirth, menopause, or terrible periods, or endometriosis, or any of those things. The thing that a woman was supposed to do was to keep quiet, knuckle down, get on with it.

'The other day, I was talking to a woman who, at sixty-nine, is seven years older than me. She said to me, "Why do you keep going on about menopause? I mean, surely, you know, people just get on with it, I just got on with it. Aren't you just spreading fear and making women unemployable?"

'As we chatted, we got a bit deeper into our own stories. And she started talking to me about how in her late forties and early fifties she'd had such severe depression that she'd had suicidal ideation. And I said, you know that terrible sense that you're out of control, and those mood swings and everything, are a symptom of menopause? And at that point, it was like a Damascene revelation for her. She actually said afterwards that the sense of shame that she'd felt for this terrible period lifted with the thought that this was something that was actually pretty normal for menopause. *That's* the generational issue. I'm glad that we're moving away from it.'

Now that I am actually in peri-menopause, I have a better perspective than I did when I'd just turned forty. There *is* an overwhelm of information, but it is better than knowing too little. In the UK, thanks to people like Mariella campaigning, there has been a huge shift in NHS policy – from 2026, menopause screening will be included in healthcare checks for women over forty. Her goal, she says, is to make sure more women know what is happening to their bodies. 'I still talk to educated, well-informed women who don't understand that peri-menopause begins for the majority of women in your early forties,' she said, 'and that a lot of the symptoms and long-term damage happens during that period of time.'

Changes are happening at an institutional level too. For the first time ever, menopause was mentioned specifically in the UK Employment Rights Bill which passed in 2025, which has been described as an enormous win for workers' rights. It means that companies with over 250 employees will have to start publishing their equality action plans, including, among many things, how they will support employees going through menopause.

Companies who continue to discriminate against women going through the climacteric by phasing them out or writing them off as 'difficult' – may find their days are numbered. In 2023, there were two landmark cases – involving Maria Rooney and Karen Farquharson – that highlighted the importance of not discriminating around the menopause. Rooney was a social worker working for Leicester City Council, and during 2017 and 2018 she was dealing with the physical and emotional effects of the menopause. She said her employer was not understanding, and when she had to take sick leave for her menopause symptoms, she was given a formal warning. Eventually she resigned and took action against her employers – the tribunal was a legal first.

Farquharson's situation was slightly different. She had worked as an office manager and took a couple of days off sick due to menopause-related symptoms. Her boss dismissed it as 'aches and pains'. She launched a grievance and was then told she was unable to work from home any longer –

and felt she was forced to resign. The panel upheld her claim of unfair dismissal.[42]

On the website Noon, Lucy Ryan wrote about the 'silent revolution' of women who are walking out of their careers, due to a combination of toxic workplaces and ageism, but also pointed out that women do have the energy and zest to step up in their careers once the worst of menopause was over. In her post, she highlighted the need for workplaces to do more to retain their talent.[43]

A greater awareness of menopause in the workplace is important to safeguard the rights of women going through it, but I also think it will help men understand how to support their partners and will empower younger women to learn more about it so that they don't end up fearing it. That way, they can engage in healthcare interventions earlier, and understand that menopause isn't the end of their career, but merely a stepping stone along the way.

* * *

Previously, my impression of the climacteric was that a demon takes over your body and you have no control over it. And that life, as you know it, is over.

What I have learned is that while no one is saying 'Whoo! Menopause was GREAT!', only around one third of women will experience the worst menopause symptoms. For the rest, while it isn't exactly sunshine and rainbows, it's not world-ending. According to the British Menopause Society, not all women will experience bad symptoms, and 80 – 90% of women will experience them within a wide spectrum of intensities.

It is also not an uncontrollable demon. Yes, it's still *technically* a demon, but some of these symptoms can be reduced with lifestyle changes (for instance, increasing physical activity and reducing alcohol intake), and some can be treated with hormone replacement therapy (HRT), which replaces the oestrogen you lose over this period of time. We are still in a time of figuring things out and there is much research still to be done. We don't yet have enough data around how much changes to our lifestyle can affect menopause symptoms because these measures have only been introduced relatively recently. And although it may not feel like it, there can be positives that come with the climacteric.

Jane McCann, who talks about a wide range of topics on her Instagram account, *The Middle Aged Goddess*, said in a post: 'I think it's human nature to gravitate towards the more negative side of things but honestly menopause has gifted me so many things. Anytime I mention that . . . people say, "well it's alright for you". In that time, I lost my sister, my marriage. I almost lost my life at one point. But what has changed for me in so many ways . . . I'm more confident, I am more willing to expand my comfort zone and try new things and meet new people and find the joy in my life that I have not ever quite felt before.'

* * *

One of the biggest problems I've faced in terms of engaging with the climacteric is the sense of being reduced to my hormones. There is an irony here, given that menopausal women were previously not listened to because it was felt they were too governed by their hormones. And now it feels as if everything we are feeling is being labelled by other women as hormone-related.

Fitness trainer Elizabeth Davies wrote a brilliant set of tweets on this, saying: 'Do you remember when, if a woman expressed annoyance, anger, frustration, sadness, any human emotion, someone would quip about it probably being her time of the month? Being reduced to my hormones in this way used to make me so angry. I think we need to be really careful not to end up in a similar scenario with the menopause transition – where we put all of someone's struggles and feelings down to peri-menopause rather than really listening, hearing, empathising and supporting.'

More than any other time in my life, this period feels as if I am walking a tightrope between the person I used to be, and the person I am becoming. While hormones are undoubtedly making the terrain of my life feel less familiar, I don't want to use them as an excuse to opt out of things. But I also don't need to course-correct by doing things I no longer want to do to 'prove' my hormones don't affect me. Because they do.

It has been a true delight to see the hair on my head thinning and somehow repositioning itself on my face in the form of some Wolverine-inspired sideburns. The rest of my symptoms, however, have so far been expressed mentally. Although I've struggled with anxiety for most of my life, the start of my peri-menopause triggered an awful bout that felt as if something deeper was swimming beneath the surface, giant stingrays carrying dread, despair and fear. That gave way to brain fog, which I initially wrote off as a heavy workload, until I realised I was groping for words that shouldn't have been lost to me. Bits of information, like the bank account number that I've known since the age of twelve, vanished into the mist.

I knew these symptoms were most likely peri-menopause, thanks to the many women raising awareness around it, and this wasn't just some terrifying, unknown thing that was happening only to me. If I wanted, I had people I could ask for help, including my own sister, who had started to experience peri-menopausal symptoms two to three years earlier.

'I didn't want to say anything,' she said carefully, when I told her, 'but it sounded like what you were experiencing was the start of peri.' I replied that I was glad she hadn't. 'I wouldn't have listened,' I said. 'I needed to come to it at the right time.'

I had been in denial about peri-menopause because I wasn't ready for it. There were so many things I still wanted to do, and I felt as if I was just starting to enjoy who I was. I didn't want my hormones to change all of that. My sister felt the same. 'I think it started for me around forty-four or forty-five,' Priya said, 'and that felt really difficult and frustrating because I was now in my stride as a mum. My kid was old enough to not be so dependent on me, we were living in a place I really loved, I was doing work I really loved, and it just felt like a real betrayal, to be struggling when everything else had slotted into place. It seemed to be like another point of transition at an age where I didn't really think I would be feeling such a transition.'

Once I realised I was in peri-menopause, however, that

presented a new set of problems. What, if anything, should I do about it? I remembered a friend mentioning that it was better to start HRT sooner rather than later. Because I wasn't in peri-menopause at the time, I had been very prickly about it, but now it seemed sensible. However, I also feared going to see a doctor because of all the horror stories I'd been told by women who felt they weren't believed or taken seriously.

Mariella gave me a shocking insight into why this was the case for a long time. 'Obviously you've got historic problems in that GPs weren't required to train in treating menopause symptoms until two years ago. So you've still got every chance of going to see a GP whose knowledge of menopause is probably as rudimentary as your own, maybe. And that is extremely problematic.'

One of the biggest problems is the long shadow cast by the 2002 Women's Health Initiative survey, which said there was a link between HRT in post-menopausal women and breast cancer. This led to a dramatic reduction in HRT being prescribed. Since then, the survey has been described as flawed, and it has been acknowledged that the risks are small.

'It's problematic because you've got a generation of GPs for whom all of that old mythology still remain as facts in their general knowledge,' Mariella continued, 'and so you still hear constantly about women being put on antidepressants, which is costing the NHS millions and millions a year and is totally unnecessary and doesn't serve any purpose. The best support during peri-menopause, and in fact, until the end of your days, is hormone replacement therapy, and we now know that as a proven scientific medical fact. But the storylines around it are still so impacted that it's really hard to change and that is one of the things that I think really needs to progress.'

I've been very lucky that I have my sister to ask for guidance, and she has empowered me to get help when I need it. But I have seen other friends locked in a battle with themselves around whether it's 'bad enough' to get help.

I could just suffer through my symptoms and would prove nothing – no one hands out medals for raw-dogging peri-menopause. Although I realise not everyone can go on HRT depending on their medical background, talking to a doctor about it should be normalised rather than suffering. In the same way that I would immediately get treatment for an eye infection or see my physio for a pulled muscle, why wouldn't I seek help for this?

When I called the GP surgery, however, I went in prepared for a fight. But when I told the receptionist what the appointment was for, her voice instantly switched to a softer, more understanding tone, from trying to find me an appointment quickly to reassuring me that I'd have a 'nice lady doctor'. When I did see the doctor, she didn't patronise me or dismiss my concerns. She listened, made sure I knew about the risks, and gave me the prescription. I was taken aback – it wasn't what I was expecting, but it was what I needed. I hope others experience the same.

* * *

When talking about the importance of women waking up to their lives, we must always look at who is leading the conversation, to make sure it isn't only helping a select few.

SHE WANTED MORE

The climacteric is an excellent demonstration of this because, in the global north, it is a conversation mainly led by white women, and that is a problem. Not because of some cutesy, tick box of representation, but because there are some fundamental, physiological differences.

Black, Hispanic and South Asian women, for instance, experience the climacteric earlier than white women.[44] Black women also carry a greater allostatic load than other women – meaning wear and tear on the body due to stress – and it is thought that long-term racial and gender discrimination, which black women face above and beyond other women, is a major contributor to this. When we then factor in menopausal symptoms, it could be argued that black women experience them more severely as a result of their greater allostatic load. The solutions, therefore, cannot come just from white women, because what works for them may not work for others.

Mariella mentioned that there have been challenges around overcoming cultural stigmas in certain communities around menopause. 'There are women who aren't represented in this huge conversation that's going on,' she said. And representation matters. Dr Nighat Arif, who is Pakistan-born and works as a GP in the UK, has been a leading voice in this space, especially for Muslim and South Asian women. She has talked about how certain aspects of menopause are not always discussed in the South Asian community, particularly around how it might affect a person's mental health and sex life. Most of these communities assume menopause is just a natural part of ageing and are apparently less likely to seek treatment for the symptoms.

Karen Arthur, who runs the account *Menopause Whilst Black*, is someone I've followed online since my late thirties. Karen has a gorgeous sense of style (I was drawn to her work because of it), and lives in East Sussex. She has two grown daughters and is sixty-three and single. 'I started speaking out because I couldn't not,' she said. 'One of the reasons I felt so alone, back when I googled menopause to find out what was going on with me, was that I saw no women of colour, no Black women, no one who looked like me.

'Every image was a white blonde with a long bob wearing beige and sitting with her head in her hands. Often the same stock image. So, I thought it was just me. I thought I was going mad. This is why I told no one at first. Then I gathered my friends around my kitchen table to share our menopause experience. When I discovered the 1994 SWAN report citing Black and Hispanic women's menopause experience and how we started our "journey" up to two years earlier in the global north than our white counterparts, I was shocked and incensed.[45] Why wasn't this common knowledge? Why didn't the doctor tell me this or why we hadn't learned it at school? It pissed me off and so I decided to talk about my menopause and my mental health.'

The response to the platform she created has been overwhelmingly positive. The podcast she created, of the same name, was the first UK podcast to address the experiences of black women experiencing menopause, and it was a space for women to realise they weren't alone. When we consider that black women bear the brunt of bias in the healthcare system (consider the higher perinatal deaths of black women), it is clearly critical to elevate their menopausal experiences so they get the care they need to even get to the baseline of care that white women receive.

Alongside highlighting the issues facing black women during menopause, Karen is also keen to talk about the power and joy. She has always loved fashion and clothes, and her Barbadian mother Joyce taught her how to sew. Her love of fashion was closely linked to her sense of validation, and when she went through a bad period of depression during menopause and subsequently left her job, she lost her spark around it. After a period of therapy and journalling, she slowly started to find her way back and began posting photos of the outfits she put together on social media, talking about what made her happy. This time, she felt it was about *her* – rather than craving the validation of others.

'Menopause, my changing body and mindset gave me the courage to be honest and authentic about what I truly loved,' she said. 'As my approach to fashion changed, it also gave me the confidence to start my own bespoke fashion business.'

Talking about the power that the climacteric can give you during this time needs nuance and care. On the one hand, you don't want to over-egg the positives, because of how differently we might each experience it – not just due to ethnicity, but also privilege. But on the other hand, from the many women I have spoken to, it can also be a galvanising time, a clearing out of what never served you, a time of renewal, even when everything in society says you are otherwise. Perhaps age clarifies what we want, and the climacteric galvanises us to engineer this change.

'I split from my abusive partner as I entered peri-menopause,' Anna said in the survey. 'I decided I'd had enough. But instead of looking after myself and seeking some healing, I poured all my energy into my career and my kids. So it was menopause and depression and realising that I had a life to live truthfully, that gave me the life I have now. I could never have predicted I would be doing the things I do now. It's not been an easy path but it's definitely rewarding.'

In the last year, I've noticed a growing number of healthcare professionals, influencers and life coaches focusing on menopausal and post-menopausal women. Some of what they say should be treated with caution, as there are people who will use the desperation of women wanting to alleviate their symptoms to sell them any old shonky shit, but there are some amazing resources out there, including menopause-specific life coaches. One of these women is Linda Husser, who lives in Atlanta and, at sixty-one years old, bursts with energy and positivity.

'Menopause is painted as a funeral procession for our womanhood,' she said. 'Of course the body changes with hot flashes, sleepless nights, mood swings and brain fog. But what if instead of treating menopause like a period of decline, we treated it like a rite of passage? A new beginning?

'For me, menopause has been an opportunity to listen to my body in a way I never have before. Instead of mourning what was, I have honoured what is becoming. We no longer have to define ourselves by fertility, by desirability or the needs of others. No one is going to give you the green light to start over, to take up space, to become who you were always meant to be. You have to decide. You have to choose yourself.'

We are in a time where there is an abundance of information, from TV shows to books to podcasts to influencers, and that is infinitely better than what came before. Speaking to women who are post-menopausal, there is a peacefulness that radiates from them – a certainty that is enviable.

'There definitely is a sense of strength, a sense of liberation,' Mariella said. 'There's something about not having periods anymore that feels like a release. The decrease in that constraining empathy and responsibility that you feel for everyone around you, particularly if you're a parent. Where you suddenly think, actually I care about *me*, I'm going to do what I feel like now. There are huge benefits to the end of our fertility and the beginning of this new phase of life, which is something that we have yet to learn to cherish.'

CHAPTER ELEVEN

REIMAGINING THE CONVERSATION AROUND AGEING

The other day, I came across the story of 61-year-old Sam Metcalfe from Saltburn, who took up skateboarding. 'I just have so much fun doing it,' she said to ITV News, 'and your age just disappears. I'm not aware that I'm 61 . . . I'm just another skater.' Although she was initially very shy about skateboarding in public, seeing other women of a similar age on social media in Australia and California doing it gave her the confidence, and now she inspires other people. Risk-taking, she says, makes her feel alive, as well as giving her joy.

Sam is part of a growing movement of women I see on my social media every week. Women who do their first power-lifting competitions in their fifties, take up karate in their seventies, breaking swimming records in their eighties. Women becoming style influencers in their sixties or starting new businesses. Women who are covered in tattoos or being playful with their hair colour; adorning themselves with jewellery. Women who were simply not visible when I was growing up.

This is good news, right? We are in an unprecedented time of role models when it comes to ageing for women. And yet the fearmongering around getting older is everywhere. The global market for anti-ageing treatments and products was valued at 47 billion US dollars in 2023, and it is set to increase to $80 billion by the turn of 2030 – and this isn't just fuelled by the over-forties market.[46]

At every turn we are told that being old and looking old are things to be avoided, and it is making us focus on the wrong things.

We think too much about the things that don't matter:
- What we look like
- How old people think we are
- Thinking that looking your age is bad
- Thinking that there is any one way to look at a particular age

And we think too little about the things that do matter:
- Being able to physically do the things we love for as long as possible
- Making decisions for our future selves that extend beyond money
- The quality of our life versus its length
- The way we recover from illness

Anti-ageing has many parallels with the conversation around diet culture, which also seeks to distract us from the important things. In the latter, you are told that having a small body will unlock acceptance, worship, delight, love. And then you are sold many, many ways to get it, without much insight into how much a fixation on a particular aesthetic may cost you in other areas of your life, especially your health. The same is true of ageing.

For most of our lives, women have been told that if we look a certain way and behave a certain way, the world will unfold for us. Only to reach midlife and find that, for most of us, it isn't true, and the booby prize is that apparently we now have to spend yet more time and money obsessing about how to claw our way back to a place of acceptance that never existed. The anger we might feel about that is a good thing. It's a fuel to push through what we really want, and to reject what we've been told about getting older.

The fight isn't easy. We live in a deeply ageist society with a tendency to discriminate against older people (according to the UN, ageism is a global challenge). Like any type of bias, ageism around getting older has a shorthand for what it denotes.[47] Frailty, being slow to learn, resistant to technology, being able to do less, looking less attractive, losing desire, emptiness, a tunnelling out of joy. The fear around getting older is implanted at an early age, both in the way older people are depicted and the vocabulary we use around it (think of things such as: *I'm being such a granny*, and *you look good for your age*), and there is a heavy emphasis on how looking old or older is the worst possible thing. No wonder most of us desperately want to escape it.

The human desire to reverse ageing is as enduring as the

one to cheat death. We may be in a time of people selling you things to hack your microbiome, telling you that you're ageing rapidly because you're too inflamed (and then selling you something to reduce the inflammation), and of next-generation facelifts that claim to reverse time. But humans have actually pursued eternal youth for centuries, from Cleopatra's donkey-milk baths to nineteenth-century skin-smoothing adhesive patches called 'Frownies'.

However, what is new is what beauty writer Jessica DeFino describes as 'aesthetic inflation'. In an essay on Gloria, a media brand that is about 'deprogramming what getting older means in a youth-obsessed society', DeFino explained it as 'the normalization of all of these beauty behaviours that we didn't really have access to 10 years ago, 20 years ago. It's changing what is considered normal as we age, what a woman in her thirties should look like, what a woman in her forties should look like. What we're seeing in the media, or in movies, and even on social media with our peers and influencers makes aesthetic modification increasingly more normal.'

There is also divisiveness around the 'right way' to age. I asked my friend and beauty editor Anita Bhagwandas, who wrote a book called *Ugly*, which looks at unpicking beauty standards. 'I think a lot of it is a distraction,' she said. 'We've created a false binary where women either age 'gracefully' (read: do nothing and accept an imposed invisibility) or are seen as vain and complicit in toxic beauty culture, and often ridiculed, because they've chosen tweakments or cosmetic surgery. But that binary is reductive and, frankly, exhausting.

'It also centres individual choices instead of questioning

why we feel the pressure to begin with. Who benefits when we fight over Botox vs bare-faced? Beauty culture, media, and aesthetics medicine are billion-pound industries that thrive off this internal conflict; it keeps us preoccupied with our faces instead of asking bigger questions about access, power, and visibility. It stops us enjoying ourselves in a great period in our lives where we've gained confidence, knowledge of ourselves and power.'

Trying to have this conversation without deferring to judgement either way is tricky. We have an anti-ageing industry growing at an alarming rate. And if we are constantly reiterating the message that ageing is bad and here is a procedure that can fix it, what does that mean for people who cannot afford expensive treatments and skincare? Where does their identity sit if these are things they cannot access, or may do at great risk to themselves if they try to get them done cheaply?

Moreover, we all have a part to play in dismantling ageism that goes far beyond our looks. Ageism affects both genders, but women are more discriminated against because of their age in the workplace, at a much earlier age than men, according to the Centre for Ageing Better.[48] They are more likely to be in poverty than older men, and there is a disparity in aesthetics. 'When does a women stop becoming desirable?' is a hotly debated topic – is it after thirty, or after forty? Older male celebrities never seem to need a caveat that 'they look good for their age' – they simply look good. Older female celebrities, however, only attain this status if they adhere to certain social norms of thinness and smooth skin, and they 'prove' their confidence by posing in a bikini.

There is, however, a growing counter-narrative to the blind acceptance that the most important thing about ageing is how you look. Whether it is down to the 'I haven't got the energy for this shit' vibe of menopausal commentators, positive ageing role models, more inclusive advertising and entertainment, or more confidence and knowledge in oneself, people are starting to realise that they have other options.

One of my favourite influencers is the Australian model Luisa Dunn, fifty-four, who became a pro-age advocate and has a full head of grey hair. She's also vocal about not having Botox or fillers. Luisa is a beautiful woman, and so she sometimes gets the 'well it's easy for you' pushback when she talks about natural ageing, but she has received thousands of ageist comments over the years, particularly about her hair, which is evidence to me that ageism is so endemic that even the Luisa Dunns of the world are not exempt from it.

It takes a lot of bravery for a person to publicly put themselves and their messaging out there daily, and I'm not here for women dragging other women down while doing nothing themselves to dismantle the system.

I asked her about her decision to age naturally, and what her views were on respecting a woman's autonomy to get cosmetic work done if she wanted. 'When you say "I do it for me," she said, 'it bypasses the intersection of community care and "coerced choice". I truly believe there are many women who truly desire to feel okay about ageing without modification, or peacefully, as I prefer to describe it.

'With the all-consuming and suffocating nature of diet culture and anti-ageing culture, we spend so much of our lives feeling like we need to fix every part of ourselves to align with a beauty standard and value system that was never built to empower us. It was built to disempower, then profit off us and rob women of their precious time, power, energy and resources. It is such a powerful distraction.

'Just imagine how many companies would go out of business if every woman over forty suddenly woke up and accepted their ageing bodies. Imagine if all of that time, energy and resources were redirected to things that truly matter – or just fighting to dismantle the systems that benefit from women's insecurities. If we truly believe that women deserve to age as freely and unapologetically as men, we should consider how our choices either reinforce and uphold the current structure or we make choices that challenge it. And we embody the change we wish to see.'

Luisa's words ring true when considering the results from my survey. In total, 56% of women said they wanted to age naturally, while 28% hadn't decided yet. Only 12% said they didn't want to age naturally. However, when it comes to getting people to think about their own feelings around ageing and to consider what they are doing and why they are doing it, I don't think referencing a collective sense of 'doing good for womankind' works. Specifics are powerful, and in this case, we need to know the details of how all this is impacting girls and young women.

The stark evidence of how it is playing out in today's world ranges from Canadian actress Shay Mitchell's kids' skincare line (which got her globally lambasted in 2025) to the tweens running around the Drunk Elephant skincare aisle in

Sephora. In 2024, there was a headline that shocked everyone: '10-year-olds obsessed with anti-ageing products!' and Dr Emma Wedgeworth, of the British Cosmetic Dermatology Group, confirmed that a growing number of adolescents were being brought in for treatment of skin problems caused by using products with far too many active ingredients intended for much older skin.

'I've spoken to twenty-somethings getting "preventative" Botox and jaw filler not because they're ageing, but because they're afraid of ever looking older,' Anita said. 'They're not just worried about wrinkles anymore ... they're pre-emptively altering their faces to avoid ageing at all. That's a profound shift. Right now, ageing feels like something we're meant to outsmart. Not embrace. Not even manage – just prevent altogether. And a lot of that is being driven by the hyper-visual, male-gaze-fuelled world we live in.

'Social media and reality TV have created a filtered, surgically tweaked ideal of womanhood that's barely human. And what's so alarming is that these aren't just pressures felt in your forties anymore – girls in their teens and early twenties are watching *Love Island* and scrolling TikTok, thinking *I need filler now so I don't look old at twenty-five*. There's no room to grow into your face. Ageing has become something to fear before you've even begun.'

One of the definitive films from my childhood was *Death Becomes Her*, a black comedy about what eventually happens in the unrelenting pursuit of eternal youth. I fear that the cautionary ending of Goldie Hawn and Meryl Streep falling down a flight of stairs, ending up in a heap of spray-painted limbs and glued-together faces, unable to die, is almost forgotten.

* * *

We live in a time where you can find someone to resonate with wherever you sit on the ageing spectrum as you get older. There are plenty of beauty experts who can guide you through the process of treatments with nuance and context, such as Sali Hughes and Caroline Hirons, just as there are people who espouse natural ageing, such as Luisa. When I recall what it was like for my mother when she was my age, it was a terrible time for body image – the hyper-thin 1990s – when there was zero visibility for anyone over forty. They were all lumped together in the same bracket as seventy-somethings, as far as fashion and advertising were concerned.

My reference points for what I might look like in my forties were therefore limited. The aesthetic I remember most strongly from my mother's generation was the sudden appearance of short hair. And not just any short hair, but brutal crops. I thought that was just what you did when you were older, because I didn't know that peri-menopause can thin your hair, or that menopause might make you sweat profusely and so shorter hair might be easier, and less upsetting. When I was in my thirties, however, things weren't that much better. I saw forty-something women on my Instagram feed suddenly switching to bright colours and bold patterns. I wasn't sure whether this was due to a need to stand out, given that women over forty felt they were becoming invisible, but it didn't feel like it fitted me either.

Although this sounds ridiculous now, I actually believed that maybe, when I turned forty, a switch would go off in my brain and I would dress completely differently from how I'd always done. This went hand in hand with people telling me that menopause would take over my life and my body. It added to the sense of being diminished and losing control over what I wanted to look like.

Needless to say, when I turned forty, none of this happened. I did see a free personal stylist at John Lewis, which helped me to expand my taste a little. But what actually gave me inspiration was drawing on a period in my life when I had most fun with my sense of style – my teenage years. Now that I had an income rather than just pocket money, I was able to buy myself nicer, more tailored versions of items, from suit jackets to PVC trousers. I chose not to resurrect harem pants, Stussy jeans, or tie-dye tops – and while I do still wear minidresses, I no longer wear skirts so short you can see my ass crack.

Although I like nice skincare, and wear light makeup most days, clothes have been the most powerful part of me feeling like myself. They reflect how masculine or feminine I might feel on any given day, how introverted I might be, how much power I need to draw from another person's gaze, or whether I want a gaze at all. When I have gone on dates, I haven't dressed for the other person, but for my own desire, my own love, my own comfort, and those things combined (not what I look like) can create the raiment of confidence.

Being able to take control of that, to shape it into armour, was a valuable lesson in realising that so much about the ageing narrative – including menopause – feels inevitable, as if some mysterious force was going to take over and carve out what makes us feel like ourselves. I say this as emphatically as possible: it doesn't have to be this way.

It's important to share our individual stories so that other women can see there are different paths and we don't all experience ageing the same way, based on a wide range of variables – from ethnicity to income to geography to biology. Social media platforms have allowed some spectacular women in their sixties to share their knowledge, wisdom, and incredible fashion with us, demonstrating that there is no statute of limitations on what you might want to wear, or how you are going to live now, or in your third act. Although it is a phrase most commonly used by baby boomers, we grew up hearing 'mutton dressed as lamb' – that awful phrase describing a woman thought to be dressing 'too young' for her age. The dismantling of that idea has been a positive shift, and women in their sixties are leading the way.

One of my favourites is 65-year-old Heidi. I was first drawn to her unique storytelling-meets-fashion videos on Instagram, where she has nearly a million followers, and then found out that she actually works as a TV screenwriter – she was an executive producer on *Baby Daddy*. No wonder her stories were so beautifully crafted, I thought. Like me, she isn't married and doesn't have children, and the trifecta was complete when I saw she has a ton of tattoos (I have a number myself and I don't often see women older than me who do). To me, her style feels effortless, but she says it wasn't always like this.

'I went through a period of not knowing what my style was,'

she said, from her home in Montecito. 'When I was fifty, and I was like, "Oh, am I too old to wear this now?", I took a look at that expression. Who made that rule up? Who is putting all these magazine articles out that say a woman has to have short hair and wear this kind of jewellery when she's this age? And I took a page out of the Gen Z girls on TikTok who just wear whatever the fuck they want. And I thought, "Well, why can't I wear whatever the fuck that I want?" I just want to be comfortable.'

'Ageism Is Never In Style' is a great platform that profiles women who push against these beliefs, and recently featured a 62-year-old woman named Yihang who quit her railway tech job to become a fashion content creator. She said: 'If you're restarting your life from sixty, start from the top. I cut off the long hair I've had for almost thirty years and dyed it blonde.'

Unlike beauty standards, fashion has felt like an important vehicle to convey more than just an aesthetic. It's about a mindset. What can you be, and who can you positively influence, if you are able to release the fear you have around ageing? That doesn't mean you have to dye your hair or get tattoos, but it does mean trying to have fun with it – and whatever that looks like is individual to you.

When Heidi started posting on social media, she just posted outfit shots on TikTok without any voiceovers. She had about 4,000 followers and the first time she told a story on a post, it went viral and she realised that what she said mattered. Although her fashion was great, the substance was in what she was saying about ageing, about being a woman without children, about not centring romantic love, about sobriety, and so on.

'The messages that I get are from people who say: *you've completely changed the way that I think about ageing* or: *I've stood up for myself on the job because of you. I broke up with a bad boyfriend because of you; I feel so much better about my own self-worth because of you.*

'I was told when I was younger that the way I was living my life wasn't the right way to be, that I was too loud and I should be married and I should have kids. So it's really nice to get to this part of my life where I'm like, okay, maybe I didn't make all the wrong decisions. And to be able to share that with other people who might be feeling the way I felt when I was thirty is so rewarding. To be able to show people that the life that they've been told is the life they're supposed to lead is just some playbook that somebody else wrote, that they don't need to follow and they'll be okay.'

Heidi is part of a wave of older influencers, which includes Gym Tan, who started posting in her sixties – first about fashion, and then about her life choices. She has talked about having her first child at the age of thirty-nine and her second at forty-four. The American designer Iris Apfel, who died at the age of 102, was famous for her distinctive, flamboyant style, but also a sense of mischievousness and delight. In the UK, one of my favourites is former fashion publisher Paula Sutton, who is in her fifties, and posts about her beautiful country life and aesthetic on Hill House Vintage. Seeing black women thrive in spaces where they have not hitherto been visible or made to feel welcome is one of my biggest joys.

Although social media often gets a bad rap, it has been one of the most powerful ways in which women in midlife, and older, have been able to own the narrative around ageing and therefore change it. And this is at a time when they are still under-represented in advertising, despite women's economic power being at an all-time high. The 2024 *Gender in Advertising Report* by CreativeX showed that older women were in fewer than 2% of all ads in 2023.[49] When they did appear in ads, it was in a stereotypical, domestic role, such as a mother or a grandmother. When we consider other identities, such as disability and race, that representation becomes even smaller. In my survey, 87% of women said they did not feel catered to by advertisers.

When former *Sunday Times* editorial director Eleanor Mills created Noon, the community for midlife women, one of the first things she did was to commission research into how women between forty-five and sixty felt about themselves and their lives. She felt strongly about highlighting the commercial potential of this market and how they were under-served, and wanted to make sure they were being represented correctly, according to how they *are*, not what some advertising exec assumes they are.

'I wanted to change the way the world looks at women over fifty,' Heidi said, 'but in the end, it's really made me change the way I look at a woman's place in this world. I'm angry about all of the lessons that I was taught when I was younger, and I get angrier every day. And so I really just want to help young women not follow some rule book they didn't write and understand that they can do whatever they want with their lives.'

SHE WANTED MORE

Women like Heidi are not only important in helping us see what could be possible in the future, but they also hold a mirror up to what our biases are like now. As much as I advocate for the dismantling of ageism, I have to acknowledge that I still simper when someone tells me I look good for my age, or I get ID'd at the supermarket while buying alcohol. There is a sad little part of me that feels a sense of triumph because I don't have grey hair yet, at the age of forty-five.

We are dealt a set of cards, and for most of our lives, it feels as if someone else holds the deck. Ageing for me is realising *I* hold the deck. I get to say which cards are important to me, and which aren't. It would be disingenuous to say how I look doesn't matter to me – it does. The key difference is knowing it isn't the only thing that matters, nor can it ever be the most important.

* * *

When I asked women in the survey which words resonated the most about getting older, 'freedom', 'contentment' and 'options to do what you want' scored the highest; then came 'peacefulness'.

Then I asked: **when you think about older women who inspire you, and what is it about how they live their life that makes you want to be them?** Guess how many people mentioned looks? Zero. The words that came through were 'confidence', 'not being bound by societal expectations', 'being unafraid' and my favourite: 'being strong but still soft'. It makes you wonder – why are we told that what we look like is so important, when actually what we want for our older age has nothing to do with that at all?

When it comes to thinking about ageing, we need to pivot the conversation away from what we are afraid of losing and think about who we want to become. What are the qualities we admire in the older women we know and how they live their lives? When we think of ourselves as older women, what kind of life do we want to be living? And get specific – from the type of home you want to what you'd like your daily routine to be.

Thinking about it may require some unlearning. I come from a culture where age is revered in a way it is not in the global west; there are many other cultures that are similar, including other parts of Asia, Africa, the Middle East, and the Caribbean. First Nation people bear an enormous amount of responsibility for mentoring younger people, passing down spiritual beliefs. In Australia, Aboriginal elders pass down their knowledge through oral tradition, and they are the keepers of knowledge about the songlines, ancient pathways that allow people to navigate the land.

In our cultures, ridiculing an older person is not acceptable, and even if you don't know them personally, you show respect. However, while I can only speak for my own culture, that reverence and respect can sometimes be to a person's detriment. I've noticed that older people are often treated as frail, simply because of their age; and they are sometimes seen as people to fuss over and do things for, even if they can do those things themselves. The natural progression is that when things are always done for them, they move less and become able to do less. And worse, they start to believe they can't do it themselves and, one day, they stop altogether.

Although I loved and respected both my grandmothers, the dominant impression I had of them towards the end was of frailty and dependence. And then, when I was growing up, I witnessed how my parents and people of their generation talked about age. It was unthinkable that someone would not dye their hair if it started going grey. All this made ageing seem like something terrible, and it took two things for me to change what I thought about it.

The first was when I spent time with Rob's older relatives in New Zealand after he passed away, and something began to shift. My first visit was a six-week trip in 2016, when I felt a tug, a need to be with my in-laws, especially because Rob had died in Auckland. This trip turned into regular visits every couple of years, and over the last decade, a new tree has taken root, which contains the relationships I have with each of them, the memories we have made, the conversations that have flowed, which has vastly outgrown the sapling of Rob's and my love.

New Zealand has a growing ageing population, and – although I know I should be wary of making generalisations – I witnessed a very similar ethos in older women I have met through my mother-in-law Prue and Rob's aunts, who range from their sixties to late seventies. They don't subscribe to the whole 'I'm old and therefore frail' mindset, and they keep active for as long as possible, whether that is chores around the house, walking their dogs or working in the garden. There is no fuss, no drama, no sense of 'we can't do it'.

Over time, I developed a gorgeous friendship with two of Rob's maternal aunts, Felicity and Gabrielle. They live separately but near each other, and they have shown me that you can craft the kind of life you want, even if life unfolds in a way you hadn't planned. Their homes are restful and peaceful and yet look very different from each other.

At the start of 2025, I went to stay with Gabrielle in her new home, where she finally had the garden she'd always wanted but had never been able to have while living in the city. I woke up early one morning and saw the bees already at work, flitting between the flowers, blooms rustling awake in the warmth of the sun. I thought, *this is it, I am surrounded by the living embodiment of someone's dream*, and it made me feel as if I could one day do the same.

The second was something I had to understand and feel in my own body, in order to realise that there was a lie around ageing. That it didn't have to default to frailty, and that I could keep trying new things until I was no longer physically capable of doing so.

* * *

When I turned forty-two, my sister and I were sitting in an open-air Muay Thai bar in Thailand, when the host made an announcement that they were looking for fighters to take part, and the winner would get a 'free bucket of booze'.

'I would love to be able to know something about martial arts in order to do that,' she said. 'Me too,' I replied. It had nothing to do with free alcohol and everything to do with having a skill. Something about it rattled around in my head, and when I got back to England, I asked my friend Aga to accompany me to a Brazilian jiu-jitsu class. My gym wasn't just for lifting weights, it was also a martial arts centre, and she was the highest-ranking woman as a black belt. I would never have tried it without her support.

Although it initially terrified me (I spent the first six months trying to talk myself out of going to a class), about a year later I added freestyle wrestling to the mix. I was watching a class one day and it seemed to me to be about flow and movement, more than it was about aggression. In the last year, wrestling has become my joy. It has shown me ways in which the human body can bend that I frankly thought were beyond me. Now, at the age of forty-five, I do three sports, which is still hilarious to me, given how much I hated it at school.

I'm not saying that, in order to figure out what ageing looks like to you, you have to take up trampolining or become an Ultimate Fighting Championship fighter, or indeed do anything physical. It's more to do with highlighting the fact that you don't have to just accept the stereotypes around ageing, and you can figure it out yourself, using your own body as a guide rather than assuming you can't do something because you have reached a certain age.

Women who reconnect with physical activity as they get older do find that it helps them feel capable and empowered, and it is a growing community. One of the forty-something women pushing this message is Elizabeth Davies, also known as 'This Woman Lifts', whose tweet about 'training for her old lady body' went viral and spawned a whole movement. Fed up with the messaging about summer bodies, she wrote: 'Training for my summer body? Fuck no! I'm training for my old lady body. Dense bones. Strong muscles. A healthy heart. Good balance. Functional independence.'

Another is Jacqueline Hooton, who is in her sixties, also known as 'Her Garden Gym', who focuses on women in their fifties and sixties, and posts well-thought-out, comprehensive messages around the importance of movement and mobility and how this translates into real life.

Singer Kim Wilde spoke on *Woman's Hour* about how much more intentional she is about her health in her sixties. 'My sixties are turning out to be one of the most glorious decades of my life for all kinds of reasons, personal reasons, physical reasons. I'm very good at looking after myself in a way I probably wasn't even in my fifties ... I want to be walking upright if I can be, I want to get out of bed okay, I don't want to live with pain. I know about all of that because I've experienced it in the last few years and overcome it just looking after myself. Sometimes you have to look at some hard truths about what you're doing, what you're not doing. I did all that and I'm getting the benefit of it now.'

One of the advocates of this in the lifting space is Catherine Duffy, who, at sixty-six, is a mother to three children and lives with her partner Elaine. She worked in social care but had to quit her job and, following a bout of depression and feeling lost, retrained as a personal trainer. Eventually, she ended up falling into powerlifting, and set up a lifting club for women. Her oldest member is sixty-one.

Talking about her clients, she said: 'Women are becoming aware of their bodies at peri-menopause and onwards.

SHE WANTED MORE

My two older female clients Ann and Glynis get very different things from it. Glynis maintains mobility, maintains strength, reduces insulin dependence levels. She had cervical cancer and returned as soon as she was fit enough following a radical hysterectomy. Ann wants to remain as strong as she can for as long as she can.'

Catherine acknowledges, however, that for some women it may feel exhausting to add yet another thing to the list. 'Middle-aged/older women are arguably even more squeezed, their work is as ever challenging, and they frequently have older parents to care for while also having children. It is an added burden of wellness, particularly in the absence of money or support or time.'

When it comes to planning for our older age or engaging in activities that help us work towards better health and freedom, the only time we're ever encouraged to do so is when it involves money.

When I was in my thirties, I was so traumatised around anything to do with money because of how poorly I'd managed my finances thus far, that even when I was out of debt in my mid-thirties, it cast a long shadow.

Eventually I did deal with it, because I read some ghastly statistic around self-employed women who don't sort out their pensions and are left in a state of penury in their old age. But it wasn't until I entered my forties that I realised that we have a society that pushes you so hard to think about your finances when you get older, but does fuck-all in every other area of your life. If I think about what a pension is, it really means putting measures in place *now*, to make sure that when you get older, you're able to enjoy a reasonable standard of living when you stop working. Money is important and necessary, but why not also have a pension mentality for other parts of your life?

So much of our planning for older age is based around fear – fear of not having enough money, fear of being able to do less, fear of being alone – that we forget what a powerful motivator joy is. Instead of asking yourself what you are afraid of when it comes to getting older, ask what kind of joy you want in your life. What would you like to do, if there were no limits? When we start from *that* place, a place of possibility, it begins to shift everything we think we know about getting older.

This doesn't mean that you're being irresponsible, or that you're ignoring the necessary practical planning around finances, but spreadsheets and numbers cannot tell the whole story. When you ask people what they want from ageing, the word that emerges most strongly is simply: possibilities.

CHAPTER TWELVE

ROLE MODELS AND CONVERSATIONS WITH OUR MOTHERS

My role models extend from complete strangers I see on social media, such as seventy-year-old women doing judo, to the older women in my life who have an unapologetic fearlessness around preserving their peace. In the middle of that are certain high-profile people I admire, and one of them is the beloved bestselling author Marian Keyes, who is charismatic, funny, relatable and warm.

Marian lives in Ireland with her husband Tony Baines, who she met when she was thirty, and she has spoken openly about her life, from her sobriety to her grief at not having children. She has sold 30 million copies of her books in thirty-three languages, and if that were me, I would be INSUFFERABLE. And yet, somehow, Marian is down to earth.

Now in her early sixties, she doesn't want to go quietly

into invisibility, but nor does she feel the need to do things to excess, like get six-pack abs or 'tour Morocco on a Harley'.

'When I thought about being in my sixties as a younger person,' she said, 'I imagined I'd be hunched over, finding it difficult to walk, and generally being unfit for purpose. Like close to death. Now that I'm here, the reality is that there are still things I want to do. I'm aware that some things are difficult physically, for instance I have arthritis and a thing with my neck, but I still feel okay. I have one life and I want to do as much with it as possible.'

Travel is still something she loves doing – she's been to Antarctica, among many other places – and she's taken up bouldering. She even thought about changing careers and did an interior design course, until she realised she didn't want to have to work for other people. As for managing other aspects of getting older, she says she gets Botox and filler and has always been open about it and will stay on HRT 'forever'.

In terms of her mindset around trying new things, she likes to keep an open mind.

'I definitely think it is never too late to start again,' she said. 'It may not go exactly how we want it to go. But at no point will you become so aged that change is pointless.' Although Marian acknowledges that she has choices and so it might be easier for someone like her, she also – to my surprise – still has self-doubt about her writing such as being out of touch with younger people. But, overall, she feels she has a lot more courage, and she feels that was partly due to the pandemic stealing a lot of time.

'There was a lot of anger in me along the lines of: don't

tell me what I can and can't do. I have become far better at defending my choices, and ignoring the people who criticise me. And about taking up space.

'If I am walking down the street, and there's like a gaggle of young men coming at me, and if they don't make way for me, I just barge straight through them. I do it fairly regularly. And they're always like, "what just happened?" And I think, I have as much right to be on the pavement as you do, you little fuckers. I will not step aside and I will not be intimidated.'

While talking to her, Marian has a similar energy to my aunts. There is softness and reflection, and there is also a bonfire of feeling – of dreams, hopes, anger and a refusal to squeeze herself in around other people. 'I have a lot of things that kind of nourish me and support me,' she said. 'I don't have that many close friends, maybe three or four. That's enough. I'm quite an introvert and they are all I need. I am able to see what I am, and the kind of person I am, and letting myself live within those parameters. When I'm not on the road working, I live such a quiet life, watching telly. That's what I want. I'll come out and see people for dinner, but I like it quiet. I like it small. I like it peaceful. And I let myself have that.'

When I asked women in the survey what kind of older women inspired them, the answers provided a star map of how we might navigate our own older age. 'They don't worry too much about what people think but are still kind,' wrote Ebony. 'And they seem to know how to enjoy their life, to have joy.'

'They are authentically themselves and they stick up for people,' added Siobhan. 'They don't take crap and call out shite like homophobia, transphobia and racism etc. They take joy in themselves; they are wise but use that to uplift others, especially other women.'

Reminding me of my aunt Meera, Teresa wrote: 'The capability to exist without constantly being productive, to enjoy peaceful time without feeling guilty about not achieving anything in particular.'

I'm not sure if I have a sharper sense of what I want from my older age because Rob's death reminded me of the years he never got, or because there was a time when I couldn't see beyond the first year of my grief, let alone imagine there might be more. But there is more. There are so many women reassuring us that it is possible.

* * *

A common reason people give for not going to therapy (apart from the cost) is that they don't want to talk about their childhood. If our childhood feels too uncomfortable to unpick, a softer way of understanding how we've been parented, especially mothered, might come through learning more about our mothers, especially what they were like as younger women. I'm not suggesting we need to painfully excavate it, and some of us may no longer have our mothers to ask, but a good starting point might be to ask yourself: what do you really know about your mother beyond her relationship with you?

Like it or not, we are defined by our mothers in one of two ways: we either spend our lives trying not to become them, or we try and become them. The journey isn't linear, and it is endlessly ironic that the people who expend the most energy trying not to become their mothers end up doing so anyway.

Despite the *Gilmore Girls* making us yearn for our mothers to be our best friends, they are not. They are so much more. There is grief, hidden pain, righteousness, intergenerational trauma and sadness, but there is also love, comfort and a sense of serenity that cannot be replicated by any other person. Not all of us are lucky enough to have a mother who made us feel safe and stable. Consider Jennette McCurdy's memoir *I'm Glad My Mom Died*, which charted her turbulent relationship with her mother when she was a child star.

One of the most poignant parts of the 'She Wanted More' survey was asking women: **when you think of your mother's generation, what are some of the different choices you want to make for yourself?** And what came back was not just what they wanted for themselves, but what they'd wanted for their mothers.

It changed according to age groups. For women in their twenties (the minimum age for the survey was twenty-five), whose mothers might be in their forties and fifties, it tended to be independence, freedom, and letting go of the 'what will people say' mentality. 'Not having a problematic relationship with weight loss' came up a lot, and a rejection of servitude to men.

Women in their thirties cited financial independence and taking care of their mental health. Not shrinking, and not sacrificing a career for kids. For women in their forties, there was an emphasis on the importance of friendship, dealing with peri and menopause, not breaking themselves trying to do it all, parenting differently, outsourcing labour, and not trauma-dumping. (All of this rings true for other people I know, of a similar age to me.)

Women in their fifties said they wanted to be healthier, to have more time for travel, to want more without apologising, to be proud of who they are and be less self-deprecating. And above all – freedom.

There were many wishes sent out like lanterns into the sky, a flame of gratitude, longing, sadness and hope:

- **Not putting all of my worth in my weight.** Ignore diet culture and beauty expectations – e.g. not starve myself, work out excessively, do yo-yo dieting. Earn enough money so that I never have to depend on a man, keep my money separate, vote with my mind and not my husband's opinion.
- **My mother wanted to act but her mother made her go to secretarial school. I've had choices and she's enabled me to do that.** I don't need to break myself and my body to serve, I don't need to sacrifice myself and my happiness. I wish she'd chosen herself and built something/some identity outside of being a mother/wife.
- **My mum is incredibly vibrant and smart and fun, but she has allowed her life to become smaller and smaller because she's afraid. I want to continue to push myself to do the things that scare me, and to try and access therapy so that I don't get trapped (although that can feel hard).** I believe in care in the community

and taking care of each other. But I do not want to be a traditional housewife who works full-time and then does a 'second shift'. I want to have time for my hobbies and interests and to rest. I also want to be more open with my friends about health issues, especially mental health and peri-menopause/menopause. I feel a lot of my mother's generation had to 'get on with it' and suffered in silence as a consequence. I want us to support each other during this next chapter of our life. And I want to start becoming stronger physically so that I am better prepared for the future stages of my life.

- **No children! Her life was miserable because financially she was forced to stay with an abusive man.** My mum never wanted kids, and she admitted she only married my dad to get away from her mother. So I have always made a conscious effort to do what I want and not what others expect.
- **My mother was not typical of her generation, having gone to an Ivy League university at a time when so many women did not choose that option or it was not available to them.** She has been a working mother for most of my life and even now, in her late 80s, often can be found at craft fairs displaying her handmade jewellery. I see a lot of her characteristics reflected in my own behaviour.

Taking the time to look at what our mothers taught us about being women means unravelling what they were taught about being women. While it can be difficult work, because some of the negative or oppressive views we have around ageing or being a woman have come from older women in our communities, taking the time to understand them can lead to compassion for them.

Compassion doesn't mean invalidating your feelings, but it is essential to understand their trauma, and our expectations of them, if we are to understand ourselves. And, if we want the cycle to be broken around existing to serve others, we have to break our thinking that the generation above us exists to serve and help us.

One of the most obvious ways to find out what women of our mothers' generations think about, or have strong feelings about, is simply to ask them. When I did this, one of the most surprising revelations was the discontent around the role of grandmother, because the stereotype is that grandmothers dote on their grandchildren and that they don't mind providing endless service for them. Sam Baker told me: 'My mum would say that everybody she knows except her has grandchildren one or two days every single week. But the difference is that they slightly resent it because they're forced into a caregiving role again.'

Some women accept it wordlessly, but others are pushing back on the idea of giving yet more of themselves when they should be shouldering less responsibility. While women in their fifties and sixties can use the word 'reclamation', we need slightly different vocabulary for women like mine and Sam's mothers who are in their seventies and eighties.

'What I see in my mum isn't a reclamation because she didn't ever have access to [that power] when she was younger,' she said. 'Getting married, having kids – it was just something you did. It's more just her realising that it's okay to not have to be doing something all the time, to not always be in service to someone all the time, to not always have to justify your time by attaching a value to it.'

I couldn't write a book about women wanting more for themselves without asking my mother what she had wanted as a young woman, and how that had changed over the course of her life.

During a visit to my parents' house on a warm summer's day, with the whine of lawnmowers in the background, we sat in the living room with a cup of tea. It was strange, feeling so formal, the Dictaphone between us. My mother is grandmother to my eleven-year-old niece Leela, and they have a strong bond and relationship. Even though Leela is based in Spain, she spends a chunk of her summer holidays with my parents, and it is precious time for all of them, especially my mother.

'Your role as a grandparent should be when you want to do it,' she said, 'not that you have taken on this additional responsibility which stops you from enjoying your life. But a lot of women seem to be taken for granted, and it is women who take on a major role in looking after the grandchildren. I get the impression that it's dumped on them without asking. Maybe their children now find it difficult to get childminders or make alternative arrangements. But grandparents now feel they can't say no because otherwise they'll feel laden with guilt. And that's not right – it's got to be at our convenience as well.'

It was a surprise for me to hear this, especially because I feel my mother often does a lot – sometimes too much in my opinion – to accommodate us when we are over. Which perhaps was a reminder that unless we get actively curious about the lives our mothers led before us, and their interior thoughts now, much of our relationship is based on our perception and assumptions about them, rather than the actual truth. Since having that conversation with her, I have tried to be more considerate about her feelings and not take her for granted. Let's just say it's a work in progress.

* * *

My life looks nothing like my mother's. The same might be said of my mother, whose life looks nothing like the life of her own mother, considering how much she and my father enjoy travelling and living life to the fullest. Her trajectory around marriage and kids, however, looked very similar to previous generations.

When my mother says something that frustrates me or feels old-fashioned, I immediately assume she isn't aware of the system she lives in. *She doesn't get it, she doesn't understand.* I don't tend to consider that perhaps it's a byproduct of the times she grew up in; I just jump to the conclusion that she isn't aware of things.

I'm sure that, in time, Leela will find whatever her mother and I say anachronistic.

When my mother and I sat down for a talk, we spoke a lot about her childhood, which involved periods of time living in Ethiopia and Ghana. She was unwell as a child, due to a hole in the heart, and as such spent a lot more time with her parents than her siblings, who were eventually sent to boarding school in India.

SHE WANTED MORE

I asked my mother whether she had a sense of what she wanted to be or do when she was a girl, and she shook her head. 'It wasn't just that I was traipsing all over the world. The way my generation was brought up, we weren't taught to think. You didn't worry because your parents looked after you. Guided you. Your parents decided what you were going to do for the rest of your life.'

Devolving your autonomy (without knowing it) to another person is almost always problematic, because their limitations will end up becoming your own. One of the hardest parts of my mother's life was not being able to go to university. It seems strange, given that both her parents were teachers, and especially when education was free. But despite her being a bright student, very good at maths and an avid reader, she wasn't encouraged to go down that path. Apparently it would have required her to board with a family that my grandfather didn't approve of, and that was the end of that.

When my mother started working in a bank, whatever salary she and her siblings earned was given to her father. She then joined the district auditors and impressed her boss. He suggested that she study for the auditor's exams, and when she asked her father about it, he said: 'Well, it's a three-year course. We'll be going back soon [to India], and you're getting married and all that.' I already knew about my mother's efforts to go to university being stymied, but I didn't know that she continued to face obstacles beyond that. It also helps to explain why she was so passionate about prioritising anything to do with education for my sister and me. At university she would give me money for books, and I now feel incredibly bad that I chose to redistribute these funds at the student union bar, specifically to Captain Morgan.

The most precious thing I learned about my mother during this chat was that, despite having every obstacle thrown at her, she didn't give up. She tried over and over again, to bring it up – asking about taking other exams, but it was hard pushing against a closed door. I could imagine my mother at that age, hopeful, passionate, striving. I imagined what could have been if marriage hadn't been the override switch to her own success. It was hard not to cry, and harder to remain impassive as she continued talking because I now knew what an act of generosity and love it was, that she raised us differently.

'I think my mother later had regrets,' she said. 'She was telling somebody about me, that I was so clever, and her biggest regret was not sending me to university. But there were good things. My parents spent more time with us than any other parents did. My father used to tell us stories at night. He taught us swimming, tennis, horse-riding. We did have fun, but the other stuff . . . I think it was just typical of the time – as their children, they just didn't think you had a brain or any feelings. You felt what they told you to feel. I don't think the relationships then between parents and children were such that you could have a true conversation about your fears.'

My mother went on to work for the tax office, set up her own business, and eventually became a project manager for the Heritage Lottery Fund (HLF). At the start of her last job, there was a part of her that felt like an outsider because

SHE WANTED MORE

everyone talked about which university they went to. She realised that she couldn't let her insecurity about that get in the way of doing a job she knew she could do.

When she left HLF to take early retirement and read all the lovely messages from people, she reflected that she'd managed teams, projects worth millions of pounds, drafted business plans, and prepared papers for trustees. 'I was one of three people chosen at the interview out of twenty-five people, most of whom had degrees,' she said. 'But this was achieved through the force of my personality. It should not be like that. Everybody should be given the opportunity to achieve their full potential.'

'I sometimes wonder if you two are what you are because of me, because of what you've gleaned about how I do things. You seem to have no fear. You have utter confidence in yourselves. You feel you can express anything and everything, and that is what it should be for anybody. And I'm glad that you are doing that at an earlier age than maybe I did.'

* * *

Learning about our mothers' stories can be a positive thing, but it's also important to understand the negative aspects. When I put a call-out to people asking them about where they first formed negative views about ageing, the majority of them cited their mothers. Likewise, a few years ago, when I was doing research into where women got their poor sense of body image, a significant number said it came from their mothers, either hearing them talk about their bodies in a shaming way or being put on diets as kids, or receiving negative comments about their weight.

I do believe that younger girls and women are more switched on to this though. In my local nail salon, I heard a mother talking about how her calves would never fit into a pair of high-heeled boots that she'd bought. 'They're ENORMOUS,' she laughed. There was a brief pause, and then her young teenage daughter sitting in the next chair pulled her up for talking badly about herself. I see it in my niece too – she has a much more advanced view of body image than either her mother or I had for most of our lives.

Baby boomer mothers were vulnerable to ageism and diet culture narratives and passed that on to us. These attitudes are still entrenched within many older women. Taking the time to understand our mothers and aunts, and grandmothers, doesn't mean you have to forgive where trauma occurred, but it's an important path to liberating yourself.

Understanding that every woman born in the last 100 years has never lived under an equitable system, that she has been given a list of rules she must follow in order to correct her flaws, and that these are the women who raised us and they didn't have the defences we have now, perhaps goes some way to releasing the power these attitudes have over us. Now, when an older woman talks badly about herself, or makes comments about my body, it doesn't make me feel angry or upset, it just makes me really sad that this stuff is still of so much importance to them. Where possible, I try to remind myself that I have a wealth of things at my disposal, from being born in a different time (where older role models exist) to having the time and money to engage with sport in my middle age. I have those things only because of people like my mother, and the women who came before me. Giving back and hyping them up is the very least I can do.

If your mother is still alive and you still have a relationship, a good place to start is to ask her who she thought she'd grow into when she was a girl. What her hobbies were. What games she liked playing as a child. What her first job was and how she felt doing it. How she feels about her relationship with your father if they are still together. What romance means to her. If she did something that felt different from the status quo, ask her why. Ask her how she feels about her life. Ask her what makes her happy. What makes her sad. How she feels about you, and what it is about you that she admires or loves.

They may feel like difficult questions, and you'll need to take care not to dredge up things that cause her pain, but asking open questions might unlock something that will make you want to hold her, and all her dreams, and offer softness and patience in the time you have left together.

CHAPTER THIRTEEN
FREEDOM, HEALING AND JOY

'Freedom and healing,' wrote the New York-based perfumer Marissa Zappas, 'especially for women, can look like madness in a world that has only ever known how to consume them.'

As I snipped the heads off the dying dahlia blooms in my garden, surrounded by calm and quiet, I reflected on these words, about what freedom means to me, and to others. Freedom to me is being able to live alone, peacefully, without anyone telling me what to do, without a man at the centre of my life. It is being able to do whatever I want, whenever I want, and mostly that is eating cold watermelon while sitting on the floor in the summer, deciding to drive to the ocean without needing to tell anyone where I am going, or wrapping myself in a blanket and reading for hours undisturbed. In a world that paws at a woman for everything she can give, freedom to me often looks like solitude.

Unlike loneliness, which is defined by a sense of isolation, solitude is chosen, and is defined by self-renewal, gathering, and recharging. When I wrote a piece called 'the restful houses of women who live alone', it had hundreds of comments and thousands of likes. One of my favourites was from Aleks Bee, who wrote: 'My mother lives alone after my wonderful dad/her husband died a few years ago. Though obviously it was hard and we miss him like hell, my mother loves her home. She has been able to redecorate how she wanted to and she has her own slow routine of drinking coffee while sitting on the patio.

'I remember seeing her socks in the kitchen (which never would have happened when my dad was alive as he was all about having things in the right place) and laughing together at the freedom she has now to just be. We joke that she runs a woman refuge, as her lady friends who are divorced or in unhappy marriages come over often for peace and quiet.'

One of the other markers of freedom for women is freedom of movement, specifically travel. Solo travel was unheard of for my mother's generation – whether undertaken alone or in groups – but it is on the increase for women. *National Geographic* wrote about how all-female solo travel might end up changing the face of the travel industry, citing the Adventure Travel Trade Association seeing a 230% increase in travel companies marketing specifically to women.[50] According to digital marketing agency Adido, 54% of British female travellers are more likely to take trips alone now than they were five years ago.[51] I've loved solo travel for over ten years now, and it is wonderful seeing women from all backgrounds – with kids, married, without – feeling brave enough to try it.

I also think about how the scale of freedom shifts and bends, simply due to latitude and longitude, and the time of our birth. Freedom is a civil right, and yet it is not a right that is equal for women. Even as I write this, in the UK we are fighting over the definition of a woman, and that fight isn't just restricting the freedom of trans women, it is also restricting the freedom of all women because it is reducing womanhood to a limited set of aesthetics and principles. We are back to performing femininity, and history tells us that women are not going to be the winners in this. A shift in geography, a few moves on the political chessboard, and my freedom could be snatched away in a moment, as it is for other women around the world.

According to the UN, over 600 million girls and women live in countries affected by conflict, and nearly three-quarters of the world's population live under autocratic rule that affects their rights and freedoms.[52] Although it is hard to talk about the lighter part of freedom when there is so much that weighs heavy, I want to focus this chapter on the interpretation of freedom in a life, the things that help to create it, and how life-altering it has been for some women, including myself, when we break through our constraints.

When I think of what freedom and healing looks like for women like me, it probably does seem like madness to the outside world. *What do you mean, you want to be alone?* Often, it may be the simple act of no longer playing the role that was assigned to you. The dutiful daughter, the all-giving mother, the goodist friend, the uncomplaining employee.

When I am asked what I want most for women, it is for every woman to be free, to exist as she wants, to be left alone, to be as silly as she likes, to not have to prove her worth to anyone, to not have to continually graft in order to be seen as a person, to pursue her hobbies. When you see a woman who is free, even for a moment, what you are seeing is her joy.

In 2025, there was a great example of this when droves of women went to see the US rapper Pitbull play live in concert dressed like him. All of a sudden, there were videos of women wearing bald caps, oversized black suits, white shirts and scrawled-on goatees, going to the gigs, dancing in the streets, in the stadiums, in train stations – challenging each other to dance-offs. It was the most beautifully bonkers movement because it wasn't orchestrated – it was just a small thing that started in the US, and spread all through the UK. When women dressed like this en masse, they felt they were together and part of something, but also that they were safe – no men were going to harass them dressed like that. Many of the comments on these videos were along the lines of: *this is what happens when women feel safe enough to experience joy.*

I think there is also freedom in having adventures. Being daring. The moment you question whether you should be stepping into a space – as long as it isn't unsafe – the answer is that you *should* take that step. There is freedom in doing things alone, and not waiting for someone else to accompany you. Think of all the things our mothers wish they had done, and what they would do with that freedom now. I only have to think of my own mother, who had a lifelong dream to go to Machu Picchu, but whose knees will no longer allow her to make the journey. I think of the unrealised dreams of our mothers, filling the sky like lanterns, illuminating the way for us.

When women tell me they couldn't possibly try something new, or they couldn't do something alone, or be alone, or try this thing that seems scary, I think – *you have no idea how much you're doing already.* You already do so much work, you already carry so much alone. You are taking care of everyone and everything, and yet the small task of taking care of yourself seems terrifying. And that is a prison in itself.

There is also freedom in letting go of patriarchal measures of success. You don't have to subscribe to their definition of power when it comes to your career. You don't have to burn your core to a cinder, trying to get up a ladder that is only designed to bear you up to a certain point.

Some might argue that freedom is a myth. That even if your rights aren't curtailed, your choices are still embedded in the lives of other people around you. But I don't think freedom is just about the ability to do whatever you want or to free yourself from responsibility for your dependants – after all, many of us love and want to care for them.

I think freedom is as much mental as it is physical, in terms of what we allow ourselves to do, the space we tell ourselves we can occupy. And freedom is held in the ability to *choose* – which is why this book exists. To give you the best chance to make those choices, to dream, to have possibilities. And if something is going to hold you back, it shouldn't be another person's idea of who you should be. If there is anything you must know by now, it is that a woman is constantly told what she is, and who she should be, and true freedom is breaking away from that.

* * *

I will say this until my last breath: one of the most important freedoms for women is financial freedom and autonomy. That doesn't mean we need to chase money or become obsessed with it – rather, we need to understand how much financial freedom impacts every single area of our lives.

Money represents independence. If you have your own money, you are the person who gets to say how your life is arranged. You are the person who retains control. Fifty years ago, you would not have been able to have a bank account without a man. You would not be able to own a house without a man. There are women right now who are trapped in awful situations and relationships because they don't have the financial freedom they need to leave. And that is why it makes me fucking apoplectic when I see twenty- and thirty-something women twirling about on social media saying what a life hack it is that a man is paying for their lifestyle. Because the shadow of the past is not that long gone. Their mothers were born at a time when the law said they could not be trusted with their own money.

Consider that in 1982 there was still at least one wine bar which wouldn't serve a woman ordering a drink alone, without the presence of a man. Solicitor Tess Gill and journalist Anna Coote took Fleet Street establishment El Vino's women ban to the Court of Appeal and got the law changed. Women have fought for equal rights which enable millennials and Gen Z women to even *have* choices around money, and to see some of them put their heads willingly back into the jaws of a beast that will crunch them up makes me despair.

Money is freedom because it allows you to leave a bad relationship if you need to. The lack of it can force you to stay in one, and sometimes that means compromising your own safety. Money allows you access to better healthcare in a system that may not take your health seriously. It can pay for medicine that can dramatically improve your quality of life. Money allows you to buy nutritious food, and do exercise that helps you build strong bones so you can have a better old age.

Women are more likely to be in poverty than men as they get older – currently in the UK, the pensions gap is around 30%. This is partly due to the gender pay gap that accumulates over a lifetime, and because, due to having children, women spend more time out of the workforce than men. That means that women who retire with an average of £69,000 in pension savings would need to work an extra nineteen years to achieve pension parity with men.

Don't let *anyone* tell you money doesn't matter. Or that it's a great idea to rely on a man financially. If a man gets angry because he wants to pay and you're uncomfortable with it – run. Money is freedom, and it is also control. Don't ever allow love to blind you and tempt you to give up your autonomy over money when it affects every single part of your life. And, if you are willingly going into a situation where you are the one not earning money in your relationship, plan for the worst-case scenario: what will I do if this person chooses to leave me? That means thinking about whether you'd need to re-enter the workforce, and asking: what financial provisions have you made (not your partner) for yourself? We all want to believe that our marriages will never fail, but they do.

'Relying on a man for your financial security . . . is a one-way ticket to hell,' said tech recruiter Dana. 'If you don't believe me, you need to ask the stay-at-home wives who were trying to re-enter the workforce after their husbands up and left them with nothing.' If you want to be a stay-at-home wife or girlfriend, she says, have a side hustle or a little business to bring in some income.

And never, ever – and I mean ever – trust a man with handling all finances because you've been socially conditioned to believe 'he's better at it' or because you find it hard. Look at those accounts, know where the money is going, and understand you have a right to it if it is your labour, and your money tied up in his.

Kristin Davis, who goes by the name 'The Manhattan Madam' on social media, often shares her insight and wisdom from her experience of working as a brothel madam with a client list of over 10,000 names. Many of her clients, she said, were married men. 'This is the harsh truth I learned from dealing with so many men. All relationships are one decision away from being over. That life that you built with someone – cars, homes, kids. Many men will lie and cheat knowing they are risking the relationship. What do you do about this? You enter the relationship smart. You create your own security. You keep in mind that love is a feeling and feelings can change.'

We are lucky to live in a time of money experts and influencers who can break down money for us in a way that is digestible. One of my favourites is financial coach Clare Seal, who started posting about her journey to dig her way out of £27K of debt on her Instagram account *My Frugal Year*. 'Without money of your own,' she told me, 'you put yourself into an incredibly dangerous position. Relationships fail all the time, and you might not have a choice in how and when yours ends. The number of women in later life poverty, because they surrendered their pension contributions to caring for children while their male partner built up a fat pension working full-time, is staggering. Often, these women also don't know that pensions should be on the table in a divorce, and miss out on a huge amount of money and security.'

Financial insecurity was the hardest lesson I learned with Rob. When he was keeping his drug addiction a secret, he accrued thousands upon thousands of pounds of debt. He kept most of it hidden because he wouldn't let me see his accounts and was so brazenly confident about having it under control. I was historically not good with money and was in a small amount of debt myself and therefore didn't feel as if I could insist.

When he finally came clean about his addiction and then the debt, I was shocked to my core. It felt as if an invisible hand was squeezing my heart, because I had relied on him to pay more of the bills as he earned more than me, and to have it all in hand. It turned out he didn't. Even worse, because of my mistakes with money, I didn't have any options. Eventually, he sold his share in a house he owned with a friend and paid off his debts. But then he did it again, accruing another £20,000 worth of debt. And at that point, along with many other reasons, I realised I could not keep doing this with Rob, because he kept lying.

The biggest thing I remember about that time was feeling trapped. At one point, it felt crushing. And I remember that when I started finally earning a decent salary, I understood that money was not frivolous or unimportant, that its ability to give you choices could even mean the difference between life and death in some cases.

That triggered a life-altering change in me. I couldn't let the narrative 'I'm terrible with money' overpower me. Over time, I worked with a money coach to figure out why money terrified me, and crucially how to feel control over it. I learned two valuable things. The first is that women tend to have less financial literacy than men.[53] This is because women are more cautious around risk-taking and investing, and that is partly due to the pervasive belief that men are somehow 'better' at money stuff than women. In a 2012 study, researchers said: 'Within couples, men tend to specialize in the handling of finances, then married, divorced and widowed women are less likely to develop their financial knowledge.'[54] I definitely internalised that belief and so I didn't take responsibility for my own choices (or lack thereof).

The second was listening to money expert Ramit Sethi, who changed my entire view of what a 'rich life' looks like (it's less to do with money and more about what is important to you and how money can facilitate that). And to confront our money beliefs. For instance, I'd always thought that you had to be rich to invest, and when I discovered that I could set up a fund with a relatively small outlay each month, it made me feel much less panicked.

When I asked Clare Seal about how she got herself into and out of debt, she said that a combination of being newly married and having two small children meant she acquired the debt by spending more than she earned. At the beginning, she felt crushed by it. 'The thing that I held close when things felt hopeless was the knowledge that, even though it was going to take a long time to fix, that time was going to pass anyway,' she said. 'Every tiny bit of progress that I made would make a difference, even if I couldn't perceive it right away.' She mentioned charities such as StepChange, Turn2Us, Income Max and Young Women's Trust, and said that you have to be compassionate to yourself.

'Our economy is built on consumer debt and women are advertised to relentlessly – usually products to "fix" whatever is supposedly wrong with us at that precise moment in time,' she said. 'There is an enormous gender wealth gap, and you have to wonder if women are being kept poor in relative terms precisely so that we have less agency in these situations. This isn't said to be defeatist, it's to encourage women to be less ashamed and more angry.

'Every step you take towards financial agency is an act of rebellion. Start by reducing your debt and building a fuck-off fund – a pot of money that allows you to reject situations that don't work for you. Educate yourself about how money works and, when you're ready, start to take some steps towards building some wealth and some real financial security.'

Undoing the shame I felt around money was essential to being able to take action, which has meant that, during lean times, I've had a financial buffer. Moreover, as someone who lives alone and pays all my own bills, I've had to become self-sufficient in a way that I previously wouldn't. However, the shadow of debt takes a long time to go, if ever. And I have the greatest empathy for women who feel stuck and hopeless, because that was me at one point.

'If you're a woman whose finances feel out of control,' Clare added, 'your first step probably needs to be addressing why you don't think you deserve money. I didn't know that I held this belief, and yet the second I started earning well, I found I had to get rid of the money immediately – often spending it on or giving it to other people. I kept myself feeling precarious because that was what I was comfortable with, what I felt I deserved. If you have low self-worth, it's almost impossible to hold on to your money.

'So, you have to find a way to convince yourself that you deserve to check your bank account and see a positive balance. You deserve to feel safe and protected from situations that don't work for you. And you don't owe anyone else your hard-earned money.'

* * *

The first time I'd ever felt financial security was when I reached a point in my corporate career where I was working as a senior manager at HuffPost and was earning a wage that

SHE WANTED MORE

helped to wipe out my debts relatively quickly. But after a year, against a backdrop of grief around losing Rob, I found it unbearable to work in that kind of environment.

It wasn't the company specifically. In so far as any kind of corporation can be benign, it was, relatively. But I grew disillusioned with the dehumanising grind of corporate life which anyone can recognise. The annual redundancies. The reshuffling of departments, which meant that you might have to report to some nepo baby and be ruled by his whims. The annual appraisals and having to manage the upset of the people I managed because they didn't get what they wanted. The bosses whose egos I had to tiptoe around. It all felt very meaningless, and perhaps it was a gift of grief that I found myself asking prematurely at the age of thirty-six: what do I want from my life?

I wanted to leave.

Leaving that kind of job security, and a path that is laid out for you, is incredibly hard. Especially if you have fought and clawed your way to a position that isn't easy for people like you to get. My decision to leave was triggered by a conversation with the then-MD of the company, who asked me to put my hat in the ring for the Editor-In-Chief position when it presented itself. 'Or at the very least, think about it as the next step for the future,' he said. I'm not saying I would have got it, but I knew then that I didn't want it. Because playing the tape forward, I realised I would never know a moment's peace. It would be constant firefighting, answering work emails on holiday, and it would mean not having a life outside work, and I didn't want it. Even thinking about it felt like incarceration.

Leaving was the best decision I could've made, and although the first two years were a slog, trying to set up my own business, often working seven-day weeks, it was worth it to have that freedom. It doesn't mean that I don't have constraints or worries – money, for instance, is a consistent worry – but it means that I have freed myself of the things that actively made me unhappy and made me feel trapped.

I know plenty of women who work in corporations and are happy. They need the consistency that corporate life affords, and they genuinely enjoy their jobs, and the buzz of power it brings. But I have seen a growing number of women who are questioning whether they need to follow the traditional trajectory of success, which can sometimes feel as if it is keyed in to a patriarchal ideal of money and power.

When we think of things such as status, it feels as if we are working to a very masculine definition, whereby your worth is measured by your job title and how much money you have. By the same token, one of the drivers around male suicide is the way men sometimes feel they have failed as economic providers. This illuminates how precarious it can be to base your identity around your professional status.

Ultimately, a job title is something that can be taken from you. And while there is a practical element to working – paying your bills, for example – it is worth considering other ways in which you can arrange your life around things that society might not praise you for, but which matter to you.

One of my favourite people who illustrates this is Saima Ishaq, a British Pakistani woman who posts videos on TikTok about her 'soft life' in London as a 42-year-old living with

SHE WANTED MORE

her parents. She came to my attention after posting a video about how she tried skateboarding, then stand-up comedy. I was intrigued by her story, especially when I found out that she's also single and childfree. Given that we both come from cultures that tend to write off women like us, I was curious about her story as she also looks like she's living her best life.

'I live with my parents still, because renting is ridiculously expensive,' she said. 'Having to live with strangers because you can't afford your own space is wild. I experienced it once in my thirties, and lived with an awful person. I absolutely do wish I had a beautiful home of my own, but it just doesn't seem likely. Maybe I'll find a path which will allow me to earn enough to buy a house . . . but not a job that will break my soul and body.'

Saima said that she can't work in one place for forty hours a week because she's done it before and has ended up resenting the job. As such, she works at various cultural arts venues, mostly evening and weekend work – which suits her as she can avoid rush-hour, and doesn't like to wake up early. 'I hate the "hustle and grind" mindset,' she said. 'I get days off mid-week, which allows me to do things at a leisurely pace, and to avoid crowds. I can watch a film in an empty cinema, I can walk around a quiet art gallery and get a table at my favourite restaurants . . . because everyone else is at work. I would hate to do this on the weekend with everyone else who is off work at the same time.'

Watching Saima document her life made me realise she's actively trying new experiences and living life in a way that many people long to, but often tell themselves they can't. Myself included.

She started posting videos of her day in a week after being encouraged by one of her younger colleagues, and then started responding to comments from people asking how it was possible for her to live this 'soft life'. The videos resonated with people. 'I'm not rich, I live with my parents, I don't go out much, I enjoy simple pleasures, I dress comfortably and repeat my outfits. I don't encourage over-consumption, I take up short-term hobbies, I'm single . . . and I feel good. People want to see this. I've heard it's called "de-influencing". I like that.'

The thing I admire most about Saima is her ability to lean into what she knows she wants to keep herself happy, versus what other people are expecting from her at that time in her life.

Her approach to work and balance also made me think about my own life. Leaving corporate life meant taking a pay cut, and my finances are more precarious. But, although I do find it hard to give myself time off and take breaks (as do many freelancers), the ability to not have to account for my time is something that is fundamentally important to the happiness of my life. And it's important to remember that this is about perception – what seems valuable to me may feel worthless to you.

'I've been told I don't "live in the real world",' said Saima, 'which I don't understand. My life isn't a mirage, it's real. I was made to feel that because I'm not struggling, I have no real say or input into any conversation . . . that I must struggle to experience real life. I reject this notion.'

SHE WANTED MORE

When we consider this within the context of Marissa Zappas' quote about freedom looking like madness, it's worth considering that your liberation hinges on your ability to let go of what others might think about your pursuits. Giving yourself the freedom to choose lightness and softness, where possible, saturates your life with joy.

One of the most delightful expressions of it is that of whimsy. For some that might be giving yourself the things you wanted as a child, but felt unable to access, or indeed reliving some of it. A close friend of mine spent her forty-fourth birthday riding rollercoasters and eating sherbet-sprinkled ice cream and loved every moment. 'Side quests' are also growing in popularity. This is when you allow yourself time to do something that doesn't have to serve an obvious purpose, from getting a licence to drive an HGV to taking a random train to explore a part of the country you haven't seen before. It doesn't even have to involve money – it could be something as simple as walking around the city looking for blue plaques that begin with the letter 'B' or seeing how many conversations you can start with a stranger. (As an introvert, I won't be doing the latter, obviously.)

My side quest in the last year has been taking up wrestling. When I am rolling around on a mat, I feel like a kid. I hadn't ever expected to have that feeling again. There are times when someone has me in a headlock that I think 'What the fuck am I doing?' but then the moment passes and I emerge sweaty, happy, laughing. Free.

* * *

One of the most inspiring stories about how we can help uplift other women to find their own sense of freedom is the tale of Asma Khan. Most people remember her story after she appeared on Netflix's *Chef's Table* in 2019, and those who have been to her supper clubs and restaurant have seen the magic of what she has created up close.

I first heard of her in 2013, at the dinner table of mine and Rob's friend George, sitting in his immaculate flat in Brixton, ahead of what was going to be an epic seven-course Sicilian seafood feast served on Christmas Eve. 'Her name is Asma,' George said as Rob rooted around in the fridge for a bottle of wine, 'and her biriyani is exquisite.' If I was going to take a food recommendation from anyone, it was going to be George. He worked as a top food consultant and cooked us the most beautiful meals from scratch, hunting for ingredients in small, specialist delis.

Asma comes from a royal Bengali-Rajput family. As a child, she was seen as a bit troublesome because she liked to play cricket out on the streets, which was considered unseemly for a girl. Her parents were not critical of her, however, even though other people in their social circle were. They told her parents that she was too fat to get married, that she should go on a diet – which they ignored. Looking back, she realises that she survived a lot by being in that deeply feudal, patriarchal set-up.

When she did get married, she moved to the UK with her husband, who was given a teaching job. Over time, she had two sons and studied to become a lawyer, getting a doctorate. Although she had never learned how to cook while she'd lived in India, she missed the dishes that reminded her of home and taught herself with the help of an aunt.

In 2012, when she was forty-three, she started to host her own supper clubs at home, initially inviting the housewives she'd met at her children's schools, many of whom were also immigrants. As word of mouth spread, restaurateur Vivek Singh came to visit, and he gave her his seal of approval. It is all the more remarkable that Asma did this in secret – her husband had no clue about it, until her children outed her because they didn't like strangers being in the house.

Although she had nowhere to host the supper clubs, she didn't give up – and I find it all the more impressive that she persisted, because pushing against your family's wishes is hard at the best of times. It is even harder when you grow up in a culture where the opinion of your family rules your world.

Eventually she was given a pop-up residency in a Soho pub in London. She called it the Darjeeling Express, and when lauded restaurant critic Fay Maschler gave her a glowing review, her star was in the ascendant. She eventually went on to launch her own restaurant, which is permanently packed out and frequented by A-list celebrities.

However, what makes Asma special isn't her trajectory from cooking at home to cooking for the King and Queen. It is that her kitchen is all-female, composed of grandmothers and mothers, immigrants and women who have found purpose and a home in her team. It has been described as a social project, a changemaker, and it is.

Asma has always been an advocate for representation, and she felt very strongly that women were seen as cooks, and men were chefs. She wanted to change the story, starting with the women who worked in her kitchen.

'When I see the look in their eyes,' she said, talking about her team, 'I see the confidence. I see the way they walk. That they look people in their eye and are not looking down, and just that itself, is a huge thing. It is more powerful, more satisfying than anything that has happened for me.'

Asma told me a story, about a mistake she had made in the early days of the restaurant, when she accidentally opened the booking system on the evening of the Lakshmi Puja, a holy day of celebration during Diwali. An evening when her staff would have been at home, preparing for it.

'We had sold out every table,' she said, 'and I was so scared. I told everybody, this is what happened, and I don't know what to do. And no one said anything to me. They just kept working. Then I saw them remove their phones from the kitchen because they must have been getting so many missed calls from home. At the end of service, I was frantic, because I had ruined all their plans. I came up and apologised. And one of the oldest members of our team said: 'Which goddess will I worship when my temple is here?'

'For all the traditional upbringing they had, that someone could say this, that she saw the kitchen as her temple, I realised how far she had come. From the time when she would not look at me in the eye, she would stand when I walked into the room and keep standing and not sit with me and eat or drink tea, because the tradition of hierarchy of status and class was so ingrained in her. I wept so much because that night I realised that she and all the other women had made that journey and understood that, tradition aside, this was their career, their future, and there was passion and pride in all their eyes. I could not breathe because I realised that she had broken her chains.'

Asma paused, her voice breaking at the poignancy of it all, and took a moment to gather herself. When she eventually looked up, she said: 'No one can break your chains for you. You've got to break them yourself, including the chains that you tie around yourself. And it doesn't mean you get rid of the things that are important to you. I'm a traditional person, and there are things that are still very important to me culturally, and traditionally. But like these women, I'm holding on to what is precious to me. And I'm also stepping away from the things that are tying me down.'

* * *

Throughout my life, I have felt connected to a network that is both visible, and not. I am a tree, my loved ones are my root system, and our memories together are the branches that grow strong and thick, even in high winds. But they are not my entire world. Somewhere out there, held under the same sky, grounded in the same soil is . . . you. We might be strangers, but we understand the shorthand of how to protect each other, how to uplift each other, how to free each other. Though we may be strangers in passing, on a train, in the street, we know something of each other's existence. That isn't nothing.

When I consider how much in this world strives to control women, and when I think of what women achieve despite this, of how we dream of silliness and joy and ambition and adventure, I think we are nothing short of spectacular. It feels appropriate, then, to finish with one final story, about a woman's journey that sprang out of nothing but a sense of: why not me?

First, some context. Among South Asians, we have a joke, which is: brown people don't do camping, and we don't ski. We don't tend to camp because not enough time has passed between colonialism and us to make sleeping in a tent an attractive or cute thing. We want mattresses and four sturdy walls. And a ceiling. We also don't ski, and maybe that is changing for Gen Z and Alpha, but for most elder millennials and Gen Xs, it's a no. (Boarding school and rich browns don't count – they are a different species with unrelatable privilege.)

We don't traditionally do cold and snowy landscapes, although this is changing as we engage more with adventure travel. For instance, I fell in love with the Arctic Circle during a trip to Sweden twelve years ago, and a recent solo group trip to Iceland which included two other Indian women I'd never met before confirmed that maybe we were drawn to the stark, pristine beauty of snow and ice. (Only as long as we were warm and firmly stuffed inside a puffer coat reaching down to our toes.)

However, it is one thing to be ferried around in a minibus with the heater blasting, and another to be on your own in the Antarctic, skiing 700 miles in forty days, carrying all your own supplies and equipment, including your tent. Which is exactly what British Army officer Preet Chandi did in 2022, making her the first woman of colour to reach the South Pole solo and unsupported.

SHE WANTED MORE

I remember reading the news at the time and jolting upright on my sofa. A couple of years ago, I interviewed Wendy Searle who had made the same journey and knew how much it had cost her mentally, emotionally and financially. It hit harder that it was a South Asian woman – our dreams feel further away, not just because of what we face in the out-side world, but the chains we wrap around ourselves because of the gendered cultural expectations that Asma alluded to.

The enormity of a woman crossing Antarctica isn't just about the endurance required for its terrain or even its extreme location. It's what it symbolises when we think about things such as exploration, adventure and frontiers.

For a long time, Antarctica was referred to as 'a woman who needed conquering', Regina Clery wrote in a review titled *Antarctica – the Woman and the Quest for a Polar Career*. 'In the 1900s Antarctica is referred to in personal accounts and expedition diaries as a more "aloof, virginal woman to be won through chivalrous deeds" (Leane 2009). [. . .] after the war of 1945 men saw Antarctica as a "testing ground for manly character".'[55]

It was felt to be a place that women couldn't endure physically as well as men. Women who'd wanted to go there faced great barriers of exclusion, and even if they were qualified for expeditions, were less likely to be selected than men.

It is hard enough for women, then, but for someone who looked like me? It seemed impossible.

Preet joined the army at the age of twenty-seven and was the first in her family to get a degree. She'd done various endurance challenges over the years and started thinking about her next challenge. 'I genuinely started by typing into Google, "How do you get to Antarctica?"' she said. 'Growing up, I didn't see people who looked like me doing things like this. I wasn't part of the adventure world and didn't realise it was something that could be for me. But I got to a point where I wanted to do something big, and something completely outside my comfort zone. I wanted to see what I was capable of, and I wanted to challenge the idea of who belongs in these spaces. The polar world felt so far removed from everything I knew and that's exactly why I went after it.

'For me, it was so much bigger than just skiing across ice. I carry my culture, my heritage, and everyone who's ever been told they don't belong, with me. I wanted to show that it doesn't matter what you look like, where you're from, or even if you know nothing about the subject, you can start from anywhere.'

She took unpaid leave from the army to do her first expedition, but eventually had to leave to pursue her challenges full-time. In January 2023 she did the longest solo unsupported one-way ski expedition by female and male – 922 miles in seventy days. And at the end of the same year, took the female speed record to the South Pole, covering 700 miles in thirty-one days.

At the age of thirty-seven, Preet has four Guinness World Records, acquired in the space of four years, and none of it has been easy – not the mental load, nor the practical load of trying to fund her challenges. But there is one thing that makes it worthwhile. 'It's not just about polar exploration,' she said, 'it's about showing that we can break boundaries, that we don't have to follow the script. I've had letters, messages, drawings, even little girls dressing up as me for school projects. That representation matters. It tells the next generation, "You belong here too." And that's why I keep going.'

Most of us will never get to the Antarctic, but I believe there is a lesson for us all to learn here. In the past, men looked to conquer the Antarctic to highlight their own sense of grandiose achievement, to prove their own exceptionalism. Today, women look to the Antarctic to find the grit within themselves, but also to light the way for others, to be the torch in the dark, to tell you to back yourself even when you cannot see the way, and to have faith and keep going. It is an act of generosity, not dominance.

'Dreaming big is about pushing beyond the limits you've been told exist by others or even by yourself,' Preet said. 'I'd say start small but start. You don't need all the answers before you begin. It's okay to be scared; I was. It is okay to do it scared. You grow in the discomfort. And don't wait for permission to take up space. Take it.'

I wonder what it is like to be Preet, to face the expanse of Antarctica, so far from home. To feel the wind around her neck, the exhaustion in her bones, flecks of ice under her nails. To look out and see only herself reflected back in the snowy vastness, and to know that while only she can propel herself forwards, she doesn't do it alone. She carries with her the dreams of so many women and girls, the love from her family, the strength from people she has never even met but who know her story, who will her onwards.

It is a metaphor for us all: choosing yourself because, in

the end, who else can build your future for you? But know that doing so doesn't mean doing it alone, and that love and community is a meltwater from many different sources that will carry you through to an ocean of beautiful experiences, if you are lucky.

As we reach the close, I can't help but reflect on all the women I've met along the way. Women who understood the lesson early, women who came to it later. Women who were stuck and lost and scared, and found a way through, somehow. Women who thought they couldn't possibly be happy again, or create anything of value, or exist without another person, and found that they could. Although every story is different, and the bars of the prison change shape, if there is anything to be drawn from these collective stories, it is that women have been and will continue to be magnificent in a world that is designed to shred their sense of self from the very beginning.

When I falter and start doubting myself, thinking I couldn't possibly do some impossible-sounding task, or I can't make a change, or I tell myself that I'm hopeless, there is one thing that always helps.

In grief, the thing that kept me afloat was anchoring myself to my loved ones. I did not drown because they did not let me. They held on fast, when all I wanted to do was sink beneath the waves. I didn't live *for* them, I lived because I thought, if they are holding on so tight, maybe they believe in a different future for me, even if I can't see it myself. Maybe there is something about me that is worth holding on to, if they love me so fiercely.

SHE WANTED MORE

And when the grief started to lift, and life became full with different people and choices, I realised that the anchor needed to change. That it needed to come from within, even when I felt lost and stuck within myself. *Especially* when I felt lost and stuck.

Next to my desk, there is a photo of myself, around three years old, and I'm wearing my favourite outfit – a little kilt dress. My head is angled at the camera, my eyes taking up most of my face, and there is a smile of mischief. That little girl is my anchor. She reminds me of where I have been, and she reminds me that all things are possible, even when I lose hope. When I scold myself for a mistake, I think of her. I think of whether I would ever use a sharp word on her. Whether I would ever tell her that something she is doing is hopeless, or that she shouldn't bother trying, or that she's an idiot. And I would never. I would do everything in my power to protect her, and to make sure she lived a good life, where she felt safe and loved, for as long as possible.

Then, when I consider that I would never tell a little girl that the world has limits, let alone that she should put limits on herself, I remember that photo is me. I would tell her to dream the biggest, most beautiful life she could have for herself. To flood her life with the smallest of joys that will puddle into an ocean. And even when she is going through something terrible, to the point where she cannot see any hope, I would hold her hands and tell her: did you know that true darkness doesn't exist? That even in the deepest cave, or a cosmic void far away in space, there is always a faint trace of light? Hold on to that light – remember it is there, remember no one can take it from you, even though they may try.

Because a woman in joy is an act of protest in this world of ours that tries to take it from us. And the most powerful thing is to keep dreaming. To want more than they allow you. So be a woman in joy. I want all that for you, and more.

ACKNOWLEDGEMENTS

This book has been a long time in the making, and has prompted me to look in so many different directions of the timeline to consider what is possible. One thing is for sure, however – this book wouldn't have existed without the continued support of my agent and friend Rowan Lawton, who has been one of my fiercest champions across six books, including this one. And my editor, Carole Tonkinson, who came up with the powerful title and loved the idea from the very first pitch. I wanted to thank my mother Jayalaxmi Shetty, to whom this book is dedicated, for everything, including the interview she gave for this book. Thank you to my father Ashok, who has done more than I ever realised, to help me grow into the person I am today. My aunt Meera, whose story was so generously given. Thank you to my sister Priya, who not only agreed to be interviewed for the book but was my sounding board for so much of it. Although my grandmothers Parvathy and Nagaveni aren't mentioned in the book and they passed away long ago, gratitude goes to them and all they did to give my parents the life they now have, and who loved their grandbabies.

Thank you to everyone who agreed to be interviewed, including: Sari Botton, Marian Keyes, Mariella Frostrup, Asma Khan, Betty Reid Soskin, Shahroo Izadi, Preet Chandi, Seema Anand, Sam Baker, Jennifer Cox, Sharmaine Lovegrove, Salima Saxton, Hollie McNish, Jody Day, Pragya Agarwal, Heidi Clements, Rishita Nandagiri, Karen Arthur, Catherine Gray, Catherine Duffy, Suja Vairavanathan, Clare Seal, Cindy Gallop, Lotte Jeffs, Shabana Chowdhury, Candice Brathwaite, Ashley Kelsch, Jada Butler, Margaret Soraya, Katariina Räike, Ranji Thangiah, Laura Jane Williams, Shannon Murray, Helen Thorn, Karen Gurney, Henika Patel, Suzanne Noble, Anita Bhagwandas, Luisa Dunn, Saima Ishaq.

My friends who have gassed me up while I've tried to write this book – thank you Mal, Zekra and Zehra. Aga, you have given me one of the biggest weapons as I navigate my forties – grappling – and for this I am truly grateful! Thank you to my mother-in-law Prue Bell, and my wonderful aunts Gaby and Felicity. Thank you to Mandeep, Hester, Laura and Fipsi – you turned my life into a rainbow.

To all the women who took the survey, and who have shared your stories so generously with me over the years, I cannot thank you enough. I see you all living your lives, with your fierce little hearts, and I wish you peace and happiness. Thank you hugely to the Bonnier team behind this book, Eleanor Stammeijer, Flora Willis, Charlotte Brown,

SHE WANTED MORE

Kelly Davis, Emily Peyton, Lucy Tirahan, and Eleanor Lawlor at The Soho Agency.

Finally, to the women who read this book. This book is a love letter to you, and for you. If you want your life to change, it will change. Trust in the enquiring spirit that compelled you to read this book and know that a force in you is already working beautiful things. I have faith in you.

REFERENCES

1 https://www.unesco.org/en/articles/pollera-aconcagua-cholitas-escaladoras-brought-their-story-unesco

2 https://www.theguardian.com/news/2024/feb/01/gen-z-boys-and-men-more-likely-than-baby-boomers-to-believe-feminism-harmful-says-poll

3 https://www.lancashirebusinessview.co.uk/latest-news-and-features/male-allies-uk-launches-new-voice-of-the-boys-research-in-parliament-6822

4 https://post.parliament.uk/research-briefings/post-pn-0750/

5 https://www.tuc.org.uk/research-analysis/reports/equal-pay-day-2024-tackling-gender-pay-gap

6 European Society of Cardiology

7 https://www.businessinsider.com/dataclysm-shows-men-are-attracted-to-women-in-their-20s-2014-10

8 https://www.bbc.co.uk/future/article/20210524-the-gender-biases-that-shape-our-brains

9 https://www.bbc.co.uk/future/article/20210524-the-gender-biases-that-shape-our-brains

10 *Journal of Clinical Endocrinology & Metabolism* https://pmc.ncbi.nlm.nih.gov/articles/PMC7688018/

11 Knight Frank report 2024 https://www.theguardian.com/money/2024/feb/28/millennials-richest-generation-wealth-property

12 https://www.ons.gov.uk/peoplepopulationandcommunity/birthsdeathsandmarriages/marriagecohabitationandcivilpartnerships/bulletins/marriagesinenglandandwalesprovisional/2021and2022

13 https://www.ucl.ac.uk/news/2019/jul/less-7-couples-share-housework-equally

14 https://www.weforum.org/stories/2020/12/covid-women-workload-domestic-caring/

15 https://www.bbc.co.uk/news/world-asia-china-56178510

16 https://www.ualberta.ca/en/folio/2025/01/women-still-doing-most-of-the-housework.html

17 https://stories.avvo.com/relationships/avvo-study-men-take-blame-divorce-often-women.html

18 https://www.ons.gov.uk/peoplepopulationandcommunity/birthsdeathsandmarriages/marriagecohabitationandcivilpartnerships/bulletins/marriagesinenglandandwalesprovisional/2023

19 https://www.ons.gov.uk/peoplepopulationandcommunity/birthsdeathsandmarriages/marriagecohabitationandcivilpartnerships/bulletins/marriagesinenglandandwalesprovisional/2023

20 https://www.mediateuk.co.uk/divorce-rate-uk/

21 https://www.theguardian.com/lifeandstyle/2017/mar/19/divorce-women-risk-poverty-children-relationship

22 https://www.asian-voice.com/News/UK/British-Asians-rethinking-marriage-and-divorce

23 https://www.abc.net.au/news/2021-04-21/facing-divorce-stigma-in-south-asian-communities/100026742

24 https://pmc.ncbi.nlm.nih.gov/articles/PMC6313686/

25 https://www.psychologytoday.com/us/blog/communicating-through-change/202404/staying-together-for-the-kids

26 https://www.ipsos.com/en/data-dive-how-motherhood-viewed-around-world

27 https://www.theguardian.com/business/2022/jul/04/half-of-all-children-in-lone-parent-families-are-in-relative-poverty

28 https://www.theguardian.com/lifeandstyle/2021/jun/19/in-praise-of-fathers-the-making-of-the-modern-dad

29 https://www.ons.gov.uk/peoplepopulationandcommunity/birthsdeathsandmarriages/conceptionandfertilityrates/bulletins/childbearingforwomenbornindifferentyearsenglandandwales/2023

30 https://www.cambridge.org/core/journals/ageing-and-society/article/caught-in-the-middle-in-midlife-provision-of-care-across-multiple-generations/5539D1998C15655F6955DAF902077DBB

31 https://www.pewresearch.org/social-trends/2024/07/25/the-experiences-of-u-s-adults-who-dont-have-children/

32 https://www.psychologytoday.com/gb/blog/the-state-of-our-unions/202208/whats-behind-the-rise-of-lonely-single-men

33 https://pmc.ncbi.nlm.nih.gov/articles/PMC11829320/

34 https://www.theatlantic.com/ideas/archive/2025/02/wealthy-sex-party-trend/680807/

35 https://www.theguardian.com/commentisfree/2022/apr/04/myth-middle-aged-women-sex

36 https://www.theguardian.com/lifeandstyle/2017/oct/28/esther-perel-the-relationship-guru-who-thinks-infidelity-isnt-all-bad

37 https://cupofjo.com/2023/06/15/mira-jacob-author-interview/

38 https://pubmed.ncbi.nlm.nih.gov/30307808/

39 https://pubmed.ncbi.nlm.nih.gov/30601037/

40 https://www.sciencedirect.com/science/article/abs/pii/S0378512215300517

41 https://pubmed.ncbi.nlm.nih.gov/36995271/

42 https://wiggin.co.uk/insight/victory-for-menopause-awareness-landmark-cases-highlight-risks-of-menopause-discrimination/

43 https://noon.org.uk/the-silent-revolution-why-midlife-women-are-walking-out-at-the-peak-of-their-careers/

44 https://thebms.org.uk/wp-content/uploads/2023/07/20-BMS-TfC-Menopause-in-ethnic-minority-women-JULY2023-B.pdf

45 https://www.swanstudy.org/discrimination-may-hasten-menopause-in-black-and-hispanic-women/

46 https://www.statista.com/topics/10423/anti-aging/

47 https://www.who.int/news/item/18-03-2021-ageism-is-a-global-challenge-un

48 https://ageing-better.org.uk/blogs/we-must-tackle-ageism-if-we-want-achieve-gender-equality

49 https://learn.creativex.com/gender-in-advertising-2024

50 https://www.nationalgeographic.com/travel/article/how-women-only-tours-are-reshaping-the-way-we-travel

51 https://www.adido-digital.co.uk/blog/how-solo-female-travel-is-becoming-popular/

52 https://www.unwomen.org/en/news-stories/feature-story/2025/02/womens-rights-in-2025-hope-resilience-and-the-fight-against-backlash

53 https://pmc.ncbi.nlm.nih.gov/articles/PMC3462438/

54 https://onlinelibrary.wiley.com/doi/10.1111/j.1745-6606.2011.01221.x

55 https://ir.canterbury.ac.nz/server/api/core/bitstreams/96c91ee6-e254-4633-a5ed-a8115d377110/content